Criminal Justice
Recent Scholarship

Edited by
Nicholas P. Lovrich

A Series from LFB Scholarly

Juvenile Incarceration and Reentry
A Photovoice Study

Casey R. Shannon

LFB Scholarly Publishing LLC
El Paso 2013

Library of Congress Cataloging-in-Publication Data

Shannon, Casey R., 1982-
  Juvenile incarceration and reentry : a photovoice study / Casey R.
Shannon.
      p. cm. -- (Criminal justice : recent scholarship)
  Includes bibliographical references and index.
  ISBN 978-1-59332-579-4 (hardcover : alk. paper)
  1. Juvenile corrections. 2. Juvenile detention. 3. Juvenile
delinquents--Rehabilitation. 4. Juvenile justice, Administration of. I.
Title.
  HV9069.S493 2013
  365'.42--dc23

                                    2012040193

ISBN 978-1-59332-579-4

Printed on acid-free 250-year-life paper.

Manufactured in the United States of America.

Table of Contents

Acknowledgments

It is with sincerest gratitude that I thank the following individuals who helped me with this work: Robyn S. Hess, Maria K. E. Lahman, Kathrine Koehler-Hak, David Gonzalez, Corey D. Pierce, Rik C. D'Amato, Kevin M. Powell, Kent W. Becker, Monica Geist, Kristin L. Johnson-Schrader, David Dougherty, Claire Thomas-Duckwitz, Ronald Glazier, and William Helling.

Thank you also to the participants and those who provided donations and financial support.

CHAPTER 1
Study Overview

Youth crime is a societal issue with implications for those involved and indirectly affected. The impacts are so vast that youth crime has been identified as a national health epidemic (Nelson, 2000). Statistics identifying the scope of juvenile crime are difficult to establish and often underestimated, given that a majority of illegal activities are unidentified or go unreported. Quantifying crime rates is further complicated by changing trends and the variation that exists across jurisdictions in the manner with which they document and report illegal activity. Recent estimates indicate that approximately 1.9 million juvenile arrests were made in 2009 (Puzzanchera & Adams, 2011). The deleterious effects of crime are not isolated to those who are the immediate victims of such acts. Juvenile crime is a complex societal issue that negatively impacts the overall quality of life for everyone. The unfavorable outcomes that result suggest a problem with implications for both youthful offenders and members of mainstream society.

The number, diversity, and complexity of theories developed to explain crime and delinquency substantiates the complexity and magnitude of the problem. There is no single theory that fully explains the reasons for youth crime or the diversity of the illegal behaviors (Lawrence, 2007). Given the multitude of intricate, interconnecting systems that have the potential to mitigate or potentiate delinquent behavior, it has been impossible for researchers to identify a unique etiology of adolescent criminal behavior. Proposed theories have considered such contributing factors as learned behaviors, disability diagnosis and academic struggles, genetic or biological contributors, and immorality. The complex nature of the problem suggests that the cause is likely multidimensional. When considered together, the predominant theories provide a considerable amount of information regarding the causes of crime. One limitation is that crime is often defined in an overarching fashion, attempting to address several elements of criminality when in fact the various levels of involvement may not be caused by the same factors.

The multifaceted nature of juvenile delinquency underscores the need to further explore the associated etiological, risk, and protective factors. Individual characteristics are influential in the onset and continuation of delinquency; however, the heterogeneity of criminal involvement makes it difficult to examine such factors independent of the contexts in which an individual functions. Although one individual is not likely to be exposed to all of the associated factors, contact with multiple risk factors contributes to heightened vulnerability for delinquent involvement. Furthermore, risk factors that impact one young person are likely to differ from those of another. Youth incarceration, not unlike criminality, is a complex problem intensified by the multiple pathways that lead to juvenile delinquency (Duffy & Wong, 2003). This variability also suggests the need for multiple modalities for working with youth offenders.

Public and political perspectives represent conflicting viewpoints about how youthful offenders should be handled. Put simply, there are proponents of punishment and increasingly harsh sentences, and the counterview that advocates for early intervention, rehabilitation and family services. According to Warr (2000), public views regarding the facets of crime and justice are typically founded upon media reports on the television or in the newspaper. This presents a problem given the potential bias and misinformation portrayed in media coverage. As Lawrence (2007) pointed out, media coverage frequently includes exaggerations and overgeneralizations, and depicts these youth as dangerous, callous criminals. Similarly, Sirpal (1997) indicated that the media, general public, and law officials frequently perceive gang members as cruel, selfish, and inconsiderate persons who commit illegal acts solely for personal gain regardless of the ways their actions impact others. Therefore, it is possible that public views of youthful offenders and preferred consequences are unfounded or disproved in research and mostly opinion-based.

One of the many potential outcomes of youth arrest is incarceration. Recent estimates indicate that over 90,000 young people are confined to juvenile correctional placements annually (Snyder & Sickmund, 2006). As a result of the reform movement, today's juvenile justice proceedings typically separate youth from adults and adult facilities. It is important to consider that despite this separation, a large number of individuals under the age of 18 become involved in the adult justice system annually. Ziedenberg (2011) approximated as many as 250,000 juveniles meet this criteria, largely due to age of jurisdiction laws. Upon entrance into correctional programs, the majority of youth struggle to cope with medical, mental health, and educational difficulties.

High rates of juvenile delinquency are suggestive of ineffective and/or nonexistent prevention efforts and insufficient programming available to those youth who become incarcerated (Nelson, 2000). In fact, Champion (2007) described the structure of juvenile justice as being so disorganized that it should be referred to as a group of processes rather than a coherent system. Unfavorable outcomes for youth who come into contact with these processes include increased rates of unemployment and poverty, as well as repetition of illegal behavior, often culminating in reincarceration. From a remedial standpoint, successful rehabilitation is reliant upon inquiry regarding the differential characteristics of those youth who re-offend and those who do not, as well as the efficacy of distinctive programs afforded to youth while imprisoned and upon release (Archwamety & Katsiyannis, 1998). Given that incarceration may be the last opportunity for some to gain the essential skills needed to reintegrate into mainstream society and become productive community members or successful adults, increased information regarding the transitional needs of these youth is indeed warranted (Leone, Krezmien, Mason, & Meisel, 2005). Increased knowledge about the prevention of initial involvement in and continuation of crime may have implications for legislators, policy makers, school systems, and communities.

Bullis, Yovanoff, Mueller, and Havel (2002) highlighted the importance of gaining a more explicit understanding of the continual needs and difficulties faced by this population in order to serve them effectively. Currently, less research is available investigating reentry and recidivism from the perspective of former juvenile offenders. As a result, little is known about the process of reintegration as experienced by adolescents who have spent time in state custody.

STATEMENT OF THE PROBLEM

There is a continual need for evidence-based intervention methods designed to support the successful community return of youthful offenders. It is conceivable that some of the factors that contribute to reincarceration may be similar to those that initiate illegal behavior; therefore, gaining insight from adolescents who have been incarcerated may have implications for all prevention levels - primary, secondary, and tertiary. Available research regarding youth recidivism typically has not included youth voice and has tended to be quantitative in nature. Youth who have been incarcerated share the common experiences of engagement in illegal behaviors and loss of freedom; therefore, they have an understanding beyond those who do not share such experiences. For example, these adolescents have interacted with people at various levels of the juvenile justice process, they have been supervised with little or no access to anything beyond the walls of their placement, they have had interactions and relationships with others in similar situations as themselves, and they may have been subject to continued supervision upon return to their communities. As a result, they are likely to have a unique perspective, qualifying them as prime sources of information regarding how best to prevent juvenile crime at various levels and better help and support these young people.

Youth incarceration reflects the interplay of many difficult circumstances, often identified as risk factors, encountered by today's youth. Preventing youth from initiating criminal behavior, diversion from further involvement in illegal behaviors, and rehabilitation of youthful-offenders is warranted. In order to achieve positive change in the lives of these youth it is essential that we gain greater insight into their daily life circumstances and experiences.

NEED FOR THE STUDY

According to Fletcher (2006), the current youth voice movement seeks to attend to, reinforce, and give power to youth, thereby enabling and supporting them in their emergent efforts to make decisions, reflect, plan for action, and advocate for change throughout their lives and in their respective communities. Photovoice is a qualitative methodology that employs participatory engagement, particularly among populations that have been marginalized, by providing group members with cameras to be used as a tool to visually capture and prompt critical discussions regarding the aspects of the contextual systems in which they interact. This method has been identified as useful among persons with little money, power, or status (Wang, Burris, & Ping, 1996). Furthermore, it has been demonstrated to be effectively empowering when employed with youth participants (Strack, Magill, & McDonagh, 2004). The philosophical underpinnings of Photovoice acknowledge that persons with stigmatized social status "have an expertise and insight into their own communities and worlds that professionals and outsiders lack" (Wang & Burris, 1997, p. 370). This study presented an opportunity for a group of youth who were formerly incarcerated to counteract stereotypes and influence public perceptions about issues they perceive as important. Encouraging these youth to examine the current contexts in which they participate has the potential to empower these young adults and further facilitate personal growth. The information gathered can subsequently be used to direct supports within various contexts (e.g., school, community, home) to reduce the likelihood of reoffending and more so, actualize their potential.

PURPOSE

I collaborated with a group of young men recently released from a period of incarceration in Colorado by providing the material items, structure, and guidance for them to capture independently their experiences within the community after release from confinement. The purpose of this study was to initiate youth voice among a population that has otherwise been largely disregarded, gain knowledge of what they identify as community strengths and weaknesses that play a role in their daily lives, and to impart this knowledge to those in a position to create change, thereby advocating for such actions.

This Photovoice project sought to address the following goals: (a) enable formerly incarcerated youth to visually record and reflect upon their community's assets and needs from their viewpoint; (b) encourage critical dialogue and awareness of salient community concerns through group discussions of photographs; and (c) communicate findings, both positive and negative, to policy makers and community members as a potential catalyst for social change (Strack et al., 2004; Wang & Burris, 1994, 1997; Wang et al., 1996). The anticipated outcomes of successful participant engagement in these elements of the methodology included a gained sense of empowerment, effective appraisal of community assets and needs, and subsequent ameliorative community action (Strack et al.; Wang & Burris). In addition to advocating for community action, the information gathered during this project has the potential to expand our current knowledge of the struggles encountered by young adults, thereby supporting the development of intervention strategies and support systems to mitigate the potential unfavorable outcomes of such experiences.

THEORETICAL ORIENTATION

It may not be possible to explain criminality by use of a single theory, nor the tenets of several theories independent of one another. A multitude of factors have been identified as playing a role in juvenile delinquency and various criminological theories exist that attempt to explain the causes of crime. Given the intricate interactions and reciprocal nature of innumerable factors, it is necessary to consider the roles of many variables and their potential interconnectedness.

Explanations of illegal behavior and delinquency are classified into two broad categories – namely, "rational" and "positivist" theories (Lawrence & Hesse, 2010). Rational theories hold that people who commit crimes do so because they made a deliberate decision based on logical reasoning. According to this viewpoint, the cause of youth crime is an exercise of free will or personal choice. Conversely, positivist theories hypothesize that behaviors result from factors over which individuals have little or no control. Positivist theories have developed a variety of explanations of crime and delinquency based on individual characteristics, social processes, and political and economic facets of life (Lawrence & Hesse).

Positivist theories can be further classified into those that identify individual traits as determinants of criminal behavior and others that identify environmental factors. Theories that center on individual character traits include such things as cognitive ability, learning disabilities, and biochemical imbalances. Conversely, environmental theories of crime focus on the contributing cultural and social aspects of the contexts in which youth function. Although these theories provide foundational information regarding the potential causes of youth crime, each is narrow in scope and oftentimes excludes consideration of the likely overlap that exists. Therefore, I chose Bandura's (1986) "theory of triadic reciprocal causation" to guide the direction of this study.

According to Bandura's (1986) social cognitive theory, people do not function as entirely independent agents, nor are they the simple result of purely environmental or situational influences. "Human functioning is a product of a reciprocal interplay of intrapersonal, behavioral, and environmental determinants" (Bandura, 2006, p. 165). Triadic reciprocal causation takes into consideration the bidirectional interplay among these sets of determinants rather than conceptualizing human functioning as being formed through unidirectional forces that work from the outside in, or vice versa. The theory does not distinguish between the relative strength or power of each domain in relation to the others, but rather espouses that this process is highly situational. Furthermore, any one occurrence is not restricted exclusively to one classification (i.e., intrapersonal, behavioral, environmental), allowing for the consideration of innumerable combinations of interplay between and within each of the three areas, thus resulting in a wide range of variability of outcomes among individuals and their shared experiences. Youth who become incarcerated may share some similar characteristics in each of these three domain areas; however, the interplay among them is likely to vary greatly for each individual. When examining human functioning, triadic reciprocal determinism does not limit or narrow one's scope but instead allows for the consideration of all potential influential factors as well as taking into consideration the uniqueness of each individual's experience of this tripartite with regard to his or herself.

RESEARCH ORIENTATION AND METHODOLOGY

According to Creswell (2007), when a problem or issue exists that implies the need to understand a group or population comprehensively, a qualitative research approach may be appropriate. Such an approach allows participants to "tell the stories unencumbered by what we expect to find or what we have read in the literature" (Creswell, p. 40). Other identified reasons for conducting qualitative research include empowering participants to share their stories and simultaneously minimizing the power relationship that commonly exists in research. In their discussion of conducting research with children and adolescents, Eder and Fingerson (2002) noted that in Western societies, youth typically hold lower status and decreased power than adults. This is especially important to consider when working with youth who have been incarcerated because the power differential is twofold -- the first being their age, and the second being a member of a population who has experienced loss of freedom and is generally stigmatized. This differential may be greatened by the presence of additional characteristics such as mental health disorders or educational disabilities, ethnic minority background, or residence in impoverished communities. Creswell suggested collaborating with participants to de-emphasize the power differential between the researcher and participants.

Qualitative research seeks to understand how people conceptualize their world and their experiences, built on the assumption that reality is based upon the meanings individuals construct through social interactions (Merriam, 1998). It is guided by the belief in multiple realities (Creswell, 2007). Given the numerous pathways to youth involvement in crime, using a qualitative approach permits the consideration of a variety of distinct perspectives. Studying the phenomenon of youth crime from the participants' perspectives allows an emic approach to research. Unlike using an etic approach that attempts to build universal theories through research practices that examine several cultures from the outside seeking commonalities, this research approach seeks to discern information about phenomena from the perspective of those involved. Pike (1967) indicated that an emic approach allows a more holistic understanding of a culture, including such aspects of daily life as attitudes, motivations, interests, and personality.

Ideally, a qualitative study evolves in response to changing conditions that arise during the process and is, therefore, flexible in nature. Consistent with this concept, Wang and Burris (1997) suggested that Photovoice projects be "...creatively and flexibly adapted..." to best meet the needs of participants (p. 383). This emergent study employed a participatory action research design using the qualitative methodology of Photovoice.

Photovoice is a qualitative methodology that uses participatory engagement by having group members take photographs that are then used to prompt critical discussions about their surroundings. This method recognizes the expertise that participants have with regard to their communities and daily interactions that might otherwise go unrecognized or be inaccessible to outsiders. This approach was used to gather such information, and subsequently was used to educate policy makers and those in positions to advocate for youth and institute changes to programs, and policies affecting their re-entry into civil society. Photovoice is grounded on the theoretical underpinnings of Freire's (1970/1995/2005) approach to critical education, feminist research theory, and participatory engagement in documentary photography (Strack et al., 2004; Wang & Burris, 1997; Wang et al., 1996; Wang, Cash, & Powers, 2000).

Several aspects of Photovoice made it a powerful tool for working with this population and lead to my decision to use it for this study. First, "their familiarity with their surroundings gives community members a distinct advantage over professionals in their ability to move through the community, portray its strengths and concerns, and use grassroots voices and images to advocate policy" (Wang & Redwood-Jones, 2001, p. 561). Secondly, it has been noted that participants of Photovoice projects gained improved skills in advocating for themselves and, further, experienced a shift in self-image from being an object of policy and procedure to an active participant in this area (Wang et al., 1996, p. 1392). According to Strack et al. (2004), youth who participated in a Photovoice project were empowered as they became aware that their input and perceptions were of interest to others. Third, Photovoice projects enable participants to counteract stereotypes and simultaneously influence public opinion, which can directly and indirectly affect public policy (Wang et al., 2000). For example, one participant of the *Language of Light* Photovoice project, which explored homelessness from the perspective of persons utilizing shelters in Michigan, enlightened policy makers to the fact that although persons stay at shelters, they sometimes have as many as three jobs (Wang et al., 2000). Fourth, this method does not require that participants be able to read, write, or have attended school. This is notable given that many youth involved with the juvenile justice process display lower levels of literacy skills than their non-offending counterparts and may have experienced both intermittent and lengthy periods without formal education. Fifth, the visual image is a powerful mode of expression and communication. Eric, a 17-year-old participant of the *Flint* Photovoice project, visually depicted his experience with violence through a photograph of a bullet hole through a bus window. He supplemented this visual by stating,

> "...I can tell that the bus I ride in is always different because the bullet holes are always in different windows. Many people use public transportation, which should not be a place where you are scared. Not that riding the bus is scary, but the bullet holes are cold reminders that you never know what will happen next..." (Wang, Morrel-Samuels, Hutchison, Bell, & Pestronk, 2004, p. 913).

Finally, in my work with this population, I have consistently found that they are able to express themselves through artistic mediums, enjoy learning and using various art techniques, and possess a certain creativity or artistic talent. Consequently, the inclusion of photography was seen not only as a data collection tool, and a possible motivating factor for active participation, but also as an opportunity for the participants to gain something of value to them through their participation – namely, photography skills and experience with photographic art.

Research Questions

Wang and Burris (1997) noted the challenge and importance of using care when presenting guidelines during Photovoice trainings so as to "expand, rather than limit the perceived range of a community's assets and to avoid a language that pathologizes its members" (p. 378). During the process of qualitative inquiry, the research questions change to reflect an evolving understanding of the issue (Creswell, 2007). The foundational research questions that I set out to answer through the responses of the participants were as follows:

Q1 What community factors do youth who have been incarcerated identify as being significant with regard to becoming involved or continuing to partake in illegal activities?

Q2 What do these young adults view as the strengths and weaknesses of their communities (e.g., gang activity, community policing, availability of support groups)?

Q3 How do young people who have experienced incarceration view themselves in relation to the various contexts in which they interact (e.g., victim of violence, leader, outcast)?

Assumptions

Assumptions are inherent in qualitative inquiry (Creswell, 2007). According to this concept, the researcher holds certain beliefs that guide the study at various stages (e.g., development of research question, design rationale, choice of methodology). Explicitly stating these suppositions can afford readers to interpret the research in light of this awareness. The following assumptions were acknowledged at the outset of this study.

Personal assumptions.

1. Youth who commit crime do not do so because they are inherently bad, but rather because of a host of neurodevelopmental, psychosocial, or psychoeducational needs;

2. Youth offenders are in need of intensive, comprehensive services in the areas of prevention, intervention, rehabilitation, and family services; and

3. Youth who have been incarcerated are subject to daily life conditions that may not be conducive to a successful transition into their communities.

Methodological assumptions.

1. The youth participants would actively engage in project activities after rapport and a trusting relationship had been established among group members and between the participants and facilitators;

2. Youth would participate honestly within boundaries that maintained their safety and level of comfort, as well as that of their peers;

3. Photographs would accurately reflect community strengths and needs as perceived by each participant; and

4. The emergent design of the study would permit the development of weekly topics that adequately capture the youths' experiences.

Implications

Prior to beginning this study, I anticipated that the findings would present implications for the adults who work with youth and families, both in and outside of the juvenile justice system. First, I believed that the photographs and presentations made might provide family and community members, educators, and policy makers the possibility of viewing and perceiving the world from the viewpoint of previously incarcerated youth as opposed to seeing it from those who traditionally control the portrayal of their lives (e.g., television, newspapers, etc.). Secondly, I anticipated that the photographic component would be well received and highlight the creative talents and perspectives of the participants. Third, the method allowed for sampling of novel social and behavioral environments given the access of the participants (Wang & Burris, 1997). Fourth, I expected that community needs and assets would be identified and depicted. Fifth, it seemed probable that public opinion might be influenced, which had implications for directly and indirectly affecting policies and procedures. Sixth, this technique involved people at the grassroots level, providing an opportunity for voice where it has otherwise been unarticulated. Finally, I envisioned that the photos and discussion might stimulate community collaboration and subsequent social action.

Limitations

The following limitations were anticipated and remained true given the nature of this study and the participant population. First, the purposeful nature of choosing participants resulted in a convenience sample. Therefore, the youth who chose to participate may have been more motivated than others or represent one subgroup of this population. It was noted that participants might have chosen to participate for external rewards (e.g., to create a favorable image to juvenile justice employees); however, this did not appear to be true of any of the participants. Second, the participants were encouraged not to take photographs or share stories that might incriminate themselves or others. This may in some ways have limited the nature of the data gathered or painted only partial pictures of their lives post-return from confinement.

CHAPTER 2

Juvenile Incarceration

INCIDENCES, POPULATION, AND PURPOSE

Incidences

Youth under the age of 18 account for 16% of arrested persons in the US (Snyder, 2006). Nationwide reports of juvenile crime totals are reliably high, yet inconsistent due to varied criteria and definitions used when estimating such data. For example, the term juvenile generally refers to individuals less than 18 years of age, yet some states legally define persons as young as 16 and 17 as adults for the purposes of justice proceedings. The juvenile justice process involves an intricate network of agencies, organizations, and personnel, oftentimes operating without adequate or efficient communication or coordination, all of which function under a wide range of local, state, and federal jurisdictions (Champion, 2007). Consequently, there is considerable variation in juvenile court proceedings and imposed dispositions, thereby resulting in a multitude of potential outcomes for youth who are taken into custody or are arrested (Champion). For example, such options include, but are not limited to, detention, arrest, and referrals. From each of these, a host of recommendations, supervisory sanctions, and secure residential placements are possible. Additionally, high residential mobility and frequent reincarceration contribute further to inconsistencies.

Approximately 307 of every 100,000 adolescents under the age of 21 were confined to public and private juvenile residential placements as a result of adjudication in 2003 (Snyder &

Sickmund, 2006). This statistic must be considered in light of the fact that states have different criteria regarding the age at which an adolescent is classified as an adult for criminal prosecution. In 2004, approximately 7,083 youth under the age of 18 were also housed in adult facilities (Snyder & Sickmund). In 2009, youth in adult prisons and jails totaled approximately 10,000 (Ziedenberg, 2011). Results of a national survey of state correctional facilities and the District of Columbia revealed a total of 33,831 youth imprisoned in secure juvenile correctional settings (Quinn, Rutherford, Leone, Osher, & Poirier, 2005). These results, however, were limited to the respondents from 29 of the 42 juvenile agencies surveyed and therefore describe only a portion of this population. Individual state estimates of juveniles reportedly incarcerated evidence further discrepancies. Quinn et al. indicated a median of 509 incarcerated youth per state; individual state reports ranged from 30 to 7,827 committed juveniles. Despite variations in the number of incarcerated youth throughout the various regions of the US, this population shares certain characteristics.

Population

Youth most commonly represented within juvenile corrections are males of color between the ages of 16 and 17, many of whom come from impoverished circumstances and are eligible for special education services (Snyder & Sickmund, 1999). Most who receive special education are qualified for this service because of intellectual disabilities, learning disabilities, or documented emotional/behavioral disorders (Leone, 1994; Leone & Cutting, 2004; Quinn et al., 2005).

Although there are fewer females involved in the juvenile justice process than males, the rate of arrest for females has recently risen sharply (Champion, 2007; Snyder & Sickmund, 2006) with female arrests accounting for 30% of juvenile arrests in 2009 (Puzzanchera & Adams, 2011; Snyder & Mulako-Wantota, 2011). Female adolescents who become incarcerated are often younger than males. According to Gallagher (1999), 21.4% of incarcerated females are 13 years of age. Historically, when compared to their male counterparts, females were more likely to be arrested due to status offenses or acts determined unlawful as a result of the participant's age (i.e., consumption of alcohol under legal age, curfew violations). However, recent statistics indicate an increase in female arrest rates in several categories (e.g., simple assault, robbery; Puzzanchera & Adams, 2011; Snyder & Mulako-Wantota, 2011). Heightened rates of violent crime arrests among female arrestees have been theorized to be related to increases in female gang involvement (Champion), increasing violence among girls, and changes in policies (Cauffman, 2008). Female offending has received less attention in the research, therefore less is known about the disparities between their illegal conduct and justice system involvements than that of male counterparts. Inequalities in the rates between males and females may be the result of differentiated treatment of female offenders throughout the legal processes. According to Cauffman, females are less likely to be arrested or to be formally charged for offenses than males, though they are more likely to be confined when they are formally charged. The evidence depicting increases in female involvement with juvenile corrections highlights the need for continued research in this area, though this area is beyond the scope of the present study.

Purpose of Youth Incarceration

Public and political perspectives represent conflicting viewpoints regarding the nature of offered services and the overall mission of youth incarceration. On the one hand, support is given for juvenile correctional facilities to house offenders with the intent to punish these youth as a consequence for their commitment offense(s) (Bullis & Yovanoff, 2005; Rutherford, Nelson, & Wolford, 1985). Those who adopt this perspective are also inclined to encourage the construction of additional prisons and the implementation of increasingly rigorous penalties (Drakeford, 2002; Nelson, 2000; Rutherford et al.) based on the notion that these youth are deliberate in their intentions and, moreover, incorrigible (Huffine, 2006). Imprisonment as a form of punishment has been criticized for being largely unsuccessful at restricting the occurrence of juvenile delinquency (Macallair, 1993).

Contrasting views argue that incarceration is an opportunity for rehabilitation (Huffine, 2006). This standpoint is more likely to support the function of juvenile detention centers as being preparatory in nature - that is, offering services focused on the development of skills needed to return successfully to mainstream society and educational institutions (Leone et al., 2005). Proponents of the second view tend to place more weight on the difficulties experienced by youth. As previously noted, the heterogeneity of criminal involvement suggests that there are numerous, intertwining causes. Though one individual is unlikely to encounter all of the associated factors, contact with multiple risk factors contributes to heightened vulnerability for delinquent involvement. Therefore, examining criminal theories, contextual variables, and individual characteristics may be helpful in advancing our understanding of the phenomenon of youth crime.

THEORIES

Criminal Theories

The interactional nature of environmental and biological factors, and the numerous probable aggregating and mitigating conditions make it difficult to pinpoint the exact determinants of youth incarceration. Outcomes for these youth are further contingent upon situational variables, fortuity of life circumstances, and the youths' reactions and choices in response to these. Thus, there is considerable variation among youth who become incarcerated regarding their reasons for participating in illegal activities. Research has commonly sought to discern the causes of youth crime by narrowing the focus to particular observable contributors (e.g., biological, environmental, social) and hence developing theories to explain the occurrence of juvenile delinquency. Unfortunately, many of these theories are unidirectional in nature.

One way to gain greater insight into these theories is by their classification as either rational or positivist. Rational theory posits that the choice to engage in illegal behaviors is voluntary and logically driven based on the notion of free will (Lawrence, 2007; Shoemaker, 2000). These theories evolved not in an attempt to explain the causes of criminal activity, but rather, in support of the development of a code of conduct which deemed that the punishment for breaking a law should correspond with the act itself. At the time, punishment was thought to be an effective preventative measure, based in part on the assumption that the behavior was a rational choice (Lawrence). Contemporary social sciences challenge this conceptualization through the consideration of extenuating circumstances that influence behavior (e.g., socioeconomic status, intelligence; Shoemaker). Similarly, positivist theories hold that behavior is not freely determined, but rather the product of aggregated social and individual factors largely beyond the control of the individual (Lawrence). This perspective is more inclined to advocate for system changes, individual intervention, and place less emphasis on punishment.

When examining criminal behavior from the viewpoint of rational choice theory, there is limited need to consider factors beyond personal choice. From the positivist point of view there are numerous factors thought to be influential in such behavior. The tenets of several schools of thought have been used to explain illegal behavior. These theoretical models include, but are not limited to, biological and biosocial (e.g., chemical imbalances, genetic predisposition), psychological (e.g., personality characteristics, mental illness), social (e.g., learned behaviors), and class theories (e.g., limited educational or employment opportunities; Lawrence, 2007). Within each of these broad areas are particular theories derived from increasingly narrow variables of focus that have been explored to identify their potential influence on delinquency and crime (e.g., learning disabilities, academic achievement, intelligence). Given the intricate nature of the relationship between biological and environmental factors, and given the variation of circumstances that exists among youth who become incarcerated, choosing a unidirectional theory would have significantly limited the scope of this study. Consequently, this study was guided by Bandura's (1986) social cognitive theory of triadic reciprocal causation in conjunction with the theories upon which the methodology, Photovoice, was founded.

Triadic Reciprocal Causation

In contrast to previously discussed theories, social cognitive theory (Bandura, 1986) does not view people as entirely autonomous agents who are involuntarily shaped and controlled by external stimuli or driven exclusively by inner forces. "Rather, they serve as a reciprocally contributing influence to their own motivation and behavior within a system of reciprocal causation involving personal determinants, action, and environmental factors" (Bandura, p. 12).

Essentially, social cognitive theory espouses that a tripartite relationship exists which involves behavior, environment, and cognitions or other personal factors. These three sets of determinants are conceptualized to interact bidirectionally, thereby each operating as a partial determinant of the other. Of the three domains, none operate exclusively from the others, nor do they operate in a concurrent, holistic interaction. Bandura (1986) defines reciprocal as, "the mutual action between causal factors," specifically indicating that this does not imply that the pattern or strength of reciprocal influences is fixed (p. 23). The influence exerted by each of the three factors is not stable, but rather specific to activities, persons, and circumstances, and therefore multidetermined with great variability between individuals. Moreover, one factor can simultaneously share in different combinations of conditions producing different outcomes. Further embodied within the theory of triadic reciprocal determinism is the reciprocality that exists among and within each of the three factors. For example, within the personal factor a mutually escalating course is present between affect and thought (Bandura).

The theoretical underpinnings of interactional causal structure view behavior as a result of a duality of control between current external stimuli and previous environmental experiences. "Past experiences obviously contribute to the development of knowledge structures and self-functions that influence current perceptions, thoughts, and actions" (Bandura, 1986, p. 16). Using this premise, youth behavior can partially be viewed as a reflection of past environmental inputs. Therefore, in order to gauge an accurate conceptualization of youth crime, one must also consider the potential impacts of developmental history in combination with the three determinants of social cognitive theory (i.e., environmental factors, behavior, personal or cognitive inputs). An explanation of these factors across the various risk variables is presented next. Although discussed independently for organizational purposes, immense overlap and reciprocal interplay often exists in the lived experience of incarcerated youth.

JUVENILE CRIME AND INCARCERATION: ASSOCIATED FACTORS

External Factors

Community characteristics. Community features have been identified as contributing to adolescent outcomes by way of structural components and social processes. Previous studies have recognized compositional factors, such as low socioeconomic status, residential mobility, and cultural heterogeneity as predictors of youth delinquency (e.g., Shaw & McKay, 1969 original work published in 1942). In addition to the relationships between these factors and youth risk, it has been suggested that structural features further play a role in shaping social interactions such as parenting practices and peer associations (Chung & Steinberg, 2006). For example, poverty, which has been recognized for its relationship with delinquent outcomes, may concurrently exert influence on other social institutions in which youth function (e.g., schools), thereby indirectly transmitting certain neighborhood risk factors (Snyder

& Sickmund, 2006). Neighborhood disadvantage, as indicated by economic and employment rates, racial-ethnic diversity, and nontraditional family structure, has been noted for its association with criminal behavior among youth (Brody et al., 2001; Elliott et al., 1996).

Community members of disadvantaged neighborhoods are less likely to communicate and engage in social interactions with one another, thus hindering the development of community norms or values, including those regarding youth behaviors (Brody et al., 2001). Minimal interactions between residents can prevent the development of social networks that could otherwise potentially avert delinquent behaviors (Brody et al.; Patchin, Huebner, McCluskey, Varano, & Bynum, 2006). Consequently, the formed environment is one that inadvertently allows for the onset and persistence of delinquent behaviors characterized by violence and criminal activity.

Because the US is one of the most violent industrialized countries, American youth are exposed to violence at high rates (Scarpa, 2003). These rates have been found to be higher in low socioeconomic and urban areas than elsewhere (Campbell & Schwarz, 1996). Exposure to violence has been identified as producing potentially damaging psychosocial effects for youth such as anxiety, depression, and behavioral problems (Freeman, Mokros, & Poznanski, 1993; Scarpa). Furthermore, contact with one type of violence (e.g., media violence, domestic violence, physical harm or neglect) has been found to increase the chances of encountering other types of violence (McCabe, Hough, Yeh, Lucchini, & Hazen, 2005). In an interview with Manuel, an adolescent male who was incarcerated at the time, he described an incidence of gang violence in which he witnessed the death of a teenage friend.

> When I was inside I heard gunshots boom boom boom like three shottys goin' off and it was G firin' at them and after he shot his three rounds they uh they shot him in the chest and the face with a shotgun. I tried to go out there but I didn't want to get hit...His mom was already

out there holdin' him...That fool died in his mom's
hands.

Although Manuel's experiences may have included criminal
behavior on the part of himself or his peers, this participation
does not negate the potentially deleterious effects of such violent
encounters. It is important to note that the greater the frequency
and severity of violent encounters, the more damaging the effects
experienced by youth. Regrettably, juvenile victimization is a
common occurrence (Sullivan, Farrell, & Kliewer, 2006) and
virtually all adolescents will encounter some form of violence
either by falling victim to mistreatment or witnessing incidences
of aggression in person or in the media (McCabe et al., 2005).

Because violence exposure is heightened in urban settings,
researchers have often used these areas to examine the possible
influence on youth psychological outcomes. Freeman et al.
(1993) found that inner-city youth readily expressed feeling
afraid and anxious about nearby community violence. Youth
who reported encountering violent events presented with lower
self-esteem and greater levels of depressive symptoms as well as
concern of death or injury (Freeman et al.). Similarly, Cooley-
Qiuille, Boyd, Frantz, and Walsh (2001) found that inner-city
youth exposed to chronic community violence reported
heightened fears of potential danger, being injured, and
additional circumstances related to residing in a hostile
environment.

One way youth may cope with the psychological effects of
community violence exposure is through problem behaviors
(Patchin et al., 2006). Huffine (2006) explained that these acting
out behaviors (e.g., aggression, delinquent acts) can be
understood as an attempt to lessen the effects of emotional
discomfort. Therefore, in addition to the psychological effects,
violence exposure has been identified as a correlate of displayed
behavioral difficulties (Patchin et al.; Scarpa, 2003). For
example, McCabe et al. (2005) identified community violence
exposure as a significant predictor of heightened externalized
behaviors and conduct problems among a population of youth

between the ages of 12 and 17 over a two-year period. Similarly, DuRant, Cadenhead, Pendergrast, Slavens, and Linder (1994) found prior community violence exposure and experiences of victimization to be predictive of self-reported use of violence among African American adolescents residing in or nearby identified housing projects in an urban community.

Youth who become the target of aggression are likely to experience similar, if not worse, effects to those who have witnessed acts of violence in their community settings. The U.S. Department of Justice (2005, as cited in Snyder & Sickmund, 2006) recognizes the crimes of rape, sexual assault, robbery, aggravated assault, and simple assault as nonfatal violent victimizations. Juveniles between the ages of 12 and 17 are two to three times more likely than adults to fall victim to these types of violent acts, with male youth experiencing 50% more mistreatment than female youth (Snyder & Sickmund). Those who experience victimization as a result of community violence have a greater probability of being arrested as both juveniles and adults and, furthermore, of engaging in violent criminal activities (Widom & Maxfield, 2001). Though exposure to violence has been identified as a risk factor for later antisocial behavior, it should not be misconstrued as a direct causal effect. The authors of a recently published well-designed and carefully constructed meta-analysis concluded that, "...the relationship is most likely complicated and nonlinear," calling for research to further assess biological and social variables which may influence the relationship between exposure to violence and both prosocial and antisocial outcomes (Wilson, Stover, & Berkowitz, 2009, p. 776).

School. Frequently, youth who reach incarceration display significant academic delays in comparison to those of their school-aged peers (Baltodano, Harris, & Rutherford, 2005). Many have endured disheartening educational experiences such as poor academic achievement (Leone & Cutting, 2004; Zabel & Nigro, 1999), grade retention, and harsh disciplinary actions (Baltodano et al.; Leone & Cutting; Wang, Blomberg, & Li, 2005; Zabel & Nigro) that may contribute to a growing detachment from school. For some youth, the educational environment becomes increasingly aversive; repeated experiences of rejection essentially play a role in youth being pushed out of or feeling compelled to leave the educational system (Baltodano et al.), moving them further along a path of social troubles characterized by unemployment and criminal involvement (Jimerson, 1999). Consequently, it is conceivable to link early educational experiences with subsequent delinquency (Baltodano et al.). As previously discussed, such relationships are correlational in nature. The number of factors associated with both poor academic achievement and juvenile delinquency makes it difficult to control for such variables in order to identify causal relationships.

Poor academic achievement appears to be one dynamic in a cyclical pattern of interrelated school difficulties encountered by a number of juveniles prior to imprisonment. Students who fail to master educational curriculum are at risk of developing a negative self-concept (Brier, 1989; Zamora, 2005) and experiencing growing academic difficulties as a result of increasingly complex instruction (Nelson, 2000). Although these outcomes are not certain or all-inclusive, they reflect common experiences among struggling students. Furthermore, students who do not meet predetermined academic benchmarks may also be considered for retention and/or social promotion, both of which have been recognized by the National Association of School Psychologists (NASP) as potentially harmful interventions for students (Rafoth, 2002), recommending instead, that educators employ alternative methods to maximize the learning outcomes of students who are behind their peers (NASP, 2011a).

Commonly, youth who enter the justice system are markedly below grade level at the time of commitment (Foley, 2001). For example, students who become incarcerated perform considerably lower than their peers on standardized measures of academic achievement (Baltodano et al., 2005; Beebe & Mueller, 1993; Foley). Classroom measures concurrently support this notion; typically, these students achieve lower grade point averages (GPAs) in comparison to their non-offending counterparts (Wang et al., 2005), with as many as 72% of incarcerated delinquents having received a letter grade of "F" in at least one subject prior to incarceration (Zabel & Nigro, 1999).

Retention and/or social promotion are used by school districts as an intervention or means to remediate low academic performance among struggling students (Jimerson, 1999). Studies indicate that certain familial, demographic, and individual characteristics increase the likelihood of being held back (Meisels & Liaw, 1993; Rafoth, 2002). Perhaps unsurprisingly, these authors have pinpointed demographic factors most commonly represented in correctional facilities. Males, students of color, students with disabilities, and youth from low socioeconomic backgrounds tend to experience higher rates of grade nonpromotion. In the US, an estimated 2.4 million students are retained annually (Rafoth); 40% of juvenile delinquents reported having experienced retention in at least one grade (Zabel & Nigro, 1999).

Studies have demonstrated that retention does not, in fact, equalize outcomes between non-retained and retained students. Instead, it has been found to be generally non-advantageous by promoting uncertain academic benefit (Rafoth, 2002) or personal-social outcomes for students (Meisels & Liaw, 1993). Nonpromotion, for example, has been found to affect self-esteem negatively and increase the likelihood that a student will engage in risky behaviors and/or decide to voluntarily withdraw from school prior to graduation (Rafoth). Recent research has called for more rigorous evaluation of retention effects, suggesting that previously noted poor outcomes among retainees may reflect pre-existing vulnerabilities among the population of students most commonly retained (NASP, 2011b).

It has been suggested that in some circumstances, poor academic achievement may result in the development of negative self-confidence (Zamora, 2005). One possible way students may attempt to compensate for this is through externalized behaviors within the educational context (Zamora). Adolescents who are overage for grade tend to display higher rates of behavior problems (Byrd, Weitzman, & Auinger, 1997). Most incarcerated youth (93%) have reported being in trouble at school, with approximately 90% experiencing suspension at some point in their schooling (Zabel & Nigro, 1999). In addition to suspension, expulsion and interim educational settings are alternative ways that students are removed from the traditional school setting.

Prior to incarceration it is not uncommon for juveniles to experience numerous residential and educational placements as well as disciplinary actions that result in removal from school, potentially producing aversive consequences. For example, Teachman, Paasch, and Carver (1997) found that a student's likelihood of dropping out increases 17% for every educational relocation. High school dropouts often present with less educational bond (Marcus & Sanders-Reio, 2001). Students who enter and leave multiple schools are likely to feel less of an educational bond with these institutions, leading to the tendency to withdraw from school through behaviors such as truancy and dropping out. As these students spend greater amounts of time in unstructured settings, the possibility that they might engage in illegal behavior resulting in eventual incarceration is increased.

Family. Family dynamics have long been recognized by criminologists as influential in the etiology of delinquency (Warr, 1993). Consideration has been given to the potential intergenerational influence of criminal behavior. Additionally, parents have been regarded as prospective mediators of youth misbehavior contingent upon factors such as marital status, parenting style, parental monitoring or disciplinary practices, and familial emotional bond or attachment.

Thornberry, Freeman-Gallant, Lizotte, Krohn, and Smith (2003) hypothesized that intergenerational continuity of delinquent behavior supports the development of antisocial behaviors among young offenders. These researchers applied data drawn from the Rochester Youth Development Study, a longitudinal study beginning in 1988, to assess the intergenerational links of antisocial behavior as well as interrelated parental mediating factors that could potentially influence development. A significant, positive relationship was found between antisocial behavior exhibited by fathers during their adolescence and similar behavior exhibited by their biological sons during childhood (Thornberry et al.). Interestingly, mothers' antisocial behavior during adolescence was less related to that expressed by their biological sons during childhood and more closely associated with the parenting techniques they employed.

Murry and Farrington (2005) similarly found that separation due to parental imprisonment presented unfavorable outcomes for boys. Separation during childhood as a result of imprisonment has been found to be predictive of greater levels of delinquent behavior than separation for other reasons, such as hospitalization or death, among prisoners' sons in London (Murry & Farrington). These researchers found that 71% of prisoners' sons exhibited antisocial personality by age 32.

Parental imprisonment poses additional indirect influences on the development of delinquent behaviors in these children by altering numerous circumstances which directly shape their development. For example, having a parent in jail is likely to change childcare responsibilities and arrangements. The results of parental incarceration consequently result not only in the separation itself, but outcomes that indirectly influence the children of these parents. For this reason, familial incarceration has also been reported as a risk factor for juvenile delinquency, independent of the experience of separation. A self-report survey of incarcerated youth revealed that many had a biological family member with a history of adjudication (Zabel & Nigro, 1999). For example, these researchers found that almost 25% of biological mothers and 49% of biological fathers were reported as having a history of incarceration (Zabel & Nigro). According to Thornberry et al. (2003), "Human development takes place in the context of intertwined social relationships and the shape of one's life course is influenced by the shape of the life courses of others" (p. 172). This suggests that the behaviors and lifestyle choices of these imprisoned parents may impact those of their children. Adults who have formerly been incarcerated are likely to be unemployed, live in poverty, have low levels of academic achievement, and display psychological difficulties; these are all things that have the potential to influence youth outcomes negatively. Increased contact with a mounting number of risk factors heightens the likelihood that these youth will exhibit delinquent behaviors because these most closely reflect their life experiences (Nelson, 2000).

Parents said to have previously displayed antisocial behaviors themselves are likely to parent in ways reflective of their past experiences and their own frequent interactions with numerous factors identified as risks. For example, males who displayed antisocial behaviors during adolescence were found to utilize less effective styles of parenting with their own offspring, while females who experienced similar circumstances of emotional distance and unpredictability during childhood were found to emulate this experience by engaging in similar relational patterns with their own sons (Thornberry et al.). In general, parenting behaviors that portray warmth and consistency appear to be coupled with lower levels of delinquent behaviors (Thornberry et al., 2003). Contrary parenting styles which are more punitive or inconsistent in nature, that provide limited supervision (Murray, & Farrington, 2010) or are characterized as unreliable, dishonest, and irresponsible (Heaven, Newbury, & Mak, 2004) can contribute to the development of antisocial behaviors. Therefore, parental characteristics may have some mediating capability with regard to youth delinquency.

Walker-Barnes and Mason (2004) examined the mediating potential that parenting played with regard to problem behaviors displayed by gang-involved youth. Youth who perceived their parents as having greater levels of behavioral control (e.g., rules) were less likely to exhibit minor delinquent acts and involvement with illegal substances; in contrast, perceptions of high levels of parental psychological control (e.g., guilt, belittlement, dismissal) were predictive of increased involvement with substances. Research has supported the relationship between youth perceptions of family functioning and the emotional and behavioral characteristics that they display (Heaven et al., 2004).

One such study examined the influence of direct (i.e., imposed sanctions) and indirect (i.e., attachment) parental controls on self-reported delinquency among high school students (Burton, Cullen, & Evans, 1995). High school students' perceptions of the control exerted over their misbehavior by their parents was assessed through a self-report survey measure that asked participants whether or not their parents monitored their behavior and enforced consequences for misconduct. A significant, inverse relationship was found between direct parental control and the occurrence and frequency of youth involvement in delinquent conduct and status offenses and consumption of illegal substances. When surveyed, as many as 75% of incarcerated youth reported that their parents were divorced or never married (Zabel & Nigro, 1999). It is possible that less supervision or parental control is available in single-parent homes making this, too, a family variable related to adverse youth outcomes.

Peer relationships. Within the contexts of peer groups, adolescents develop an understanding of community norms and further acquire and practice social skills (Deptula & Cohen, 2004). During adolescence, there is a general increase in participation and expressed values for deviant behavior (Moffitt, 1993). For those youth who have encountered numerous risk factors and are therefore more prone to engage in delinquent acts, peers can exert strong influence and support for the development of antisocial behaviors. One possible explanation for this has to do with the greater degrees of positive reinforcement given for antisocial behaviors than for prosocial behaviors among delinquent peers (Dishion, Spracklen, Andrews, & Patterson, 1996). Social pressure put forth by peers has the potential to impact other youth significantly in part, due to the large time spans during which they interact (Dishion et al.). It is possible then that adolescents who are more susceptible to influence by their peers are likely to engage in peer-approved deviant behaviors more frequently (Allen, Porter, & McFarland, 2006).

According to Mears, Ploeger, and Warr (1998), the most widely recognized predictor of criminal behavior is the number of delinquent peer associations. Such associations have been linked with youth aggression and the successive development of internalized and externalized problem behaviors (Mrug, Hoza, & Bukowski, 2004). Consistent with many previously discussed risk factors, males are more likely than females to have exposure to delinquent peers (Mears et al.). One plausible explanation for the formed associations between deviant youth was proposed by Kupersmidt, DeRosier, and Patterson (1995). These researchers found that youth who shared similar demographic, behavioral, and educational traits were more likely to become friends. Conversely, youth tended to dislike or be disliked by those whose popularity status and behavioral manner differed from their own (Nangle, Erdley, & Gold, 1996).

Displayed behaviors such as aggression and withdrawal may influence the perceptions of peers (White, Rubin, & Graczyk, 2002). Nangle et al. (1996) reported that disruptive students were more frequently liked by peers who similarly displayed greater levels of non-normative behaviors such as initiating fights, being uncooperative, and displaying low levels of leadership skills. Therefore, youth with community and family risk factors predictive of delinquency are likely to become friends. Associations with violent peers have been further correlated with gang involvement (Snyder & Sickmund, 2006). These peer groups are likely to encourage the development and continuation of increasingly delinquent behaviors as opposed to those supportive of educational attainment or similar prosocial outcomes. During the school year, violent crimes committed by juveniles tend to peak during the hours just after school lets out (3 p.m. and 4 p.m.) or when youth are more likely to be together in unstructured contexts (Snyder & Sickmund). As youth become increasingly involved in misconduct and with negative peers, a growing disconnection from school is probable, diminishing the potential positive impact this context may afford. In general, peers play both a direct and indirect role with regard to an adolescent's initiation and continuation of criminal activities.

Given the numerous familial, school, and peer variables found to be related to delinquent outcomes, as well as the multiple changing and interacting ecological systems in which youth are embedded, it is difficult to identify distinct causal relationships between such factors and ultimate youth incarceration. The information gleaned from these studies provides greater knowledge regarding the circumstances that may be associated with risk and/or prediction of subsequent juvenile delinquency; however, all youth who experience one or more of these situations will not necessarily participate in delinquent behaviors or become incarcerated as a consequence.

The elements of various settings, such as interpersonal interactions, activities, and adopted roles (Bronfenbrenner, 1979), create unique interactions and outcomes. These interactions shape the youth's worldview and perceptions, and additionally have the potential to increase or decrease an individual's likelihood of committing illegal acts. According to Bandura's (1986) social cognitive theory, each individual's genetic potential, biological vulnerabilities, cognitive abilities, and related personality traits interact reciprocally with environmental settings and the factors within each context. Therefore, it is equally important to give proper consideration to the internal factors that have been found to play a role in this phenomenon.

Intraindividual Factors

Mental illness and biological vulnerabilities. The majority of youth who come into contact with the juvenile justice process display characteristics that are consistent with the *Diagnostic and Statistical Manual of Mental Disorders*, 4th edition revised (DSM-IV-TR; 2000) criteria for oppositional defiant disorder (ODD) or conduct disorder (CD). Furthermore, diagnoses common among this population include attention deficit hyperactivity disorder (ADHD), emotional/behavioral disorders, and learning disabilities. Adolescents with these disorders share similarities in areas such as impulsivity; social perception difficulties (Larson, 1988; Malmgren, Abbott, & Hawkins, 1999); suggestibility; difficulty foreseeing consequences (Keilitz & Dunivant, 1986); and struggles with conceptualization, attention, comprehension, and judgment (Brier, 1989). These disorders are typically indicative of a continuum of challenges that have the potential to impair a youth's ability to navigate his or her environment and interpersonal interactions successfully, and may concurrently result in intraindividual struggles such as depression or low self-efficacy. Furthermore, Perry (1994) noted that youth who experience traumatic experiences or inconsistent, threatening home environments may remain in a state of hyperarousal regardless of the degree of threat in a context. Behavioral symptoms of hyperarousal include defiance, impulsivity, and anxiety that may present as post traumatic stress disorder (PTSD), ADHD, or CD (Perry & Pollard, 1998). This is an important consideration because such characteristics are commonly observed among youth who become incarcerated.

Youth with and without diagnosis alike may misperceive neutral environmental stimuli as threatening. Reactions to perceived threats may not be appropriate according to the norms of the environment (e.g., talking back to a teacher) and therefore impede the adolescent's ability to function under such conditions. Despite the self-protective mechanisms these behaviors may serve, it is quite common that they are simultaneously counterproductive in interpersonal and environmental interactions (e.g., misinterpreted by a teacher as insubordination, resulting in suspension). When discussing the potential impact of mental illness in the lives and decisions of these youth, it is also necessary to keep in mind that "while not all attention deficit disorder (ADD), hyperactivity and ODD are trauma-related, it is likely that the symptoms that lead to these diagnoses are trauma-related more often than anyone has begun to suspect" (Perry & Szalavitz, 2006, p. 51).

Substance abuse and exposure. Development occurs along a trajectory beginning in utero through adulthood. Prenatal and perinatal exposure to teratogens (e.g., illicit or prescription drugs, alcohol, environmental toxins) can impair optimal development throughout the lifespan. The potential impacts include both effects that are observable at birth, such as neonatal toxicity or physical impairments, and long-term behavioral or neurodevelopmental results. In addition to the increased risk of fetal death, structural abnormalities, and possible growth deficiencies, are outcomes less readily observable and varying in severity that include a range of cognitive impairments (e.g., attention, learning, memory) and emotional dysfunction (Arnstein & Brown, 2005; Freyer, Crocker, & Mattson, 2008).

Substance use has been associated with a host of confounding factors that secondarily affect development such as polydrug use, poor prenatal nutrition, quality of caregiver environment and parenting (Arnstein & Brown). Maternal substance use has been found to be associated with childhood outcomes that include learning problems and disruptive behavior disorders (i.e., ADHD, ODD, CD), higher rates of substance abuse, and persistent legal troubles (Arnstein & Brown Freyer; Crocker, & Mattson, 2008).

Adolescents may choose to experiment or use substances illegally for numerous reasons: lack of education regarding the harmful effects, an environment or neighborhood that does not discourage or encourages use, peer pressure, and as a coping mechanism for managing uncomfortable feelings or situations. According to Perry (2004), youth disengage from the external world using numerous mechanisms. Substance abuse may be one such . example. During adolescence, the brain continues to undergo development and structural alterations. Thus, the use of drugs and alcohol during this stage can cause significant impairments in life-skills and overall functioning. Drugs and alcohol interfere with neurotransmitters and introduce chemicals into the brain that can alter developmental processes (Horton & Horton, 2005). The unfavorable effects of substance use extend beyond physical and developmental consequences to risks inherent when perception and judgment is inhibited and youth are surrounded by environmental factors commonly associated with drug and alcohol use (e.g., unsafe peers).

It is important to consider the potential impacts of substance use in the lives of young people who become incarcerated, given the potential, sometimes irreversible, deleterious impacts that enhance vulnerability of breaking the law (i.e., impaired perception, lowered inhibitions, structural damage to important brain networks responsible for functioning). It is also conceivable that a reciprocal relationship exists between drug addiction and involvement in other illegal acts. A youth's better judgment may be clouded by substance use or have developed under the premise of norms that do not align with those of mainstream society (e.g., parent minimization of drug use being wrong, gang involvement or associations, crime as a survival mechanism given harsh environmental circumstances). Furthermore, the potential monetary or substance profit is likely to make illegal acts such as theft and distributing stolen property or drugs more appealing to youth who abuse drugs.

Disorders: Emotional, behavioral, and learning. There is a high co-occurrence of mental illness diagnosis, substance use, and learning troubles among this population, all of which have the potential to powerfully impact cognitive functioning, interpersonal relationships, and the decision to partake in illegal acts. For example, students with emotional/behavioral disabilities are more likely to struggle with rule compliance and exhibit inappropriate responses to rules and regulations, thereby heightening their chances of difficulties in the learning environment and subsequent disciplinary consequences (Leone & Cutting, 2004). Disabilities commonly co-occur and share similar behavioral indicators such as difficulties with attention and emotional troubles, further compounding the struggles encountered by these youth (Lyon, Fletcher, & Fuchs, 2006).

Hypotheses have been proposed regarding the relationship between youth learning and behavioral characteristics and juvenile delinquency (Zamora, 2005). Specifically, researchers have developed theories to help explain the link between learning disabilities and juvenile delinquency. Given the co-occurrence of learning disabilities with other types of disabilities (e.g., emotional disability) and personality attributes similarly shared by incarcerated youth who have not been formally identified as having a disability (e.g., impulsivity, emotional regulation deficits, low frustration tolerance), they appear to also be applicable to incarcerated youth who do not receive services for disabilities (see Wheldall & Watkins, 2004).

Furthermore, many youth who become incarcerated, regardless of disability status, frequently exhibit psycho-educational characteristics that may be concerning. For example, Malmgren et al. (1999) pointed out that adolescents who experience frequent and/or sustained absences from school may display an underachievement profile similar to that of a peer who is learning disabled, despite not have a learning disability.

The three most often cited theories include the "susceptibility hypothesis", the "differential treatment hypothesis", and the "school failure hypothesis". According to the susceptibility hypothesis (Brier, 1989; Keilitz & Dunivant, 1986; Malmgren et al., 1999; Zamora, 2005), students with learning disabilities are more susceptible to engaging in non-normative or delinquent acts. These youth are assumed to be predisposed to becoming involved in such activities as a result of numerous personality attributes characteristic of those with learning disabilities (e.g., impulsivity, decision making difficulties, suggestibility).

The differential treatment hypothesis (Brier, 1989; Keilitz & Dunivant, 1986; Larson, 1988; Malmgren et al., 1999; Zamora, 2005) holds that youth with disabilities are treated differently than non-disabled adolescents at various stages of the legal process, resulting in greater numbers of youth with learning disabilities being jailed. This argument supposes that youth with and without disabilities engage in similar acts of misconduct at comparable rates, yet those with disabilities are arrested and/or adjudicated more regularly.

Finally, the school failure hypothesis (Brier, 1989; Keilitz & Dunivant, 1986; Larson, 1988; Malmgren et al., 1999) posits that students with learning disabilities experience school failure, which constitutes the first step along a sequential pathway ending with delinquency. A central component of this theory is that academic failure precedes criminal behavior. Poor academic achievement is postulated to contribute to the development of negative self-image, reduced self-confidence, and feelings of frustration associated with education (Brier; Keilitz & Dunivant; Larson; Malmgren et al.). These feelings are likely compensated for through externalized behaviors (Zamora, 2005). Consequences for these displayed problem behaviors (e.g., out of school suspensions) often separate students from the school environment, thereby increasing the likeliness that youth will have opportunities to become involved in antisocial activities and associate with delinquent peers (Larson). Moreover, the school failure hypothesis suggests that discouraging educational experiences support the student's progressive disengagement from school, increasing the likelihood of school dropout and again, greater potential for participation in criminal acts, and negative peer associations.

RECIDIVISM

The interplay among cognitions and personal factors, behaviors, and the environmental context of actions allows for a multiplicity of outcomes that includes initiation, continuation, and reengagement in illegal behaviors and incarceration. Conversely, some youth who spend time committed to a state facility discontinue breaking the law upon reentry into their communities; however, an individual may experience incarceration numerous times before this change in behavior patterns happens.

Youth who become incarcerated are at an increased risk of recidivism or repeated contact with juvenile justice processes. Recidivism has been defined as the repetition of unlawful conduct (Snyder & Sickmund, 2006). Similar to rates of youth crime, approximations of recidivism rates are undoubtedly underestimated given that unreported crimes are not included (Snyder & Sickmund). Documenting recidivism rates among youthful offenders can be further hindered by inefficient record-keeping and limited interjurisdictional record-sharing common among participating organizations (Champion, 2007). For example, if an adolescent's first offense is dismissed or diverted to a conditional program, it may not be recorded. Therefore, when considering placement and other considerations for juveniles, they may be viewed as a first-offender when they are actually repeat offenders whose first offense went undocumented. Furthermore, recidivism rates are estimated using various criteria such as re-arrest, reconviction, new adjudication, return to correctional commitment, correctional status changes (e.g., moving from standard to intensive probation), and violations of probation program conditions. These definitional variations signify additional challenges to estimating recidivism rates among youth who offend.

Given that different jurisdictions define and thus record recidivism in various ways, a national recidivism rate for juveniles is non-existent (Snyder & Sickmund, 2006). However, we can gain some awareness of recidivism rates by looking at individual state records, such as those of Colorado, where this study was conducted. The state of Colorado established the following definitions of recidivism in fiscal year (FY) 1999-2000. Pre-discharge recidivism is defined as "a filing for a new felony or misdemeanor offense that occurred prior to discharge from the Department of Youth Corrections (DYC)" that also includes time on parole status (Research & Evaluation Unit, DYC, 2007). Whereas, post-discharge recidivism is, "a filing for a new felony or misdemeanor offense that occurred within one year following discharge from DYC" (Research & Evaluation Unit, DYC). Of those youth discharged during the State of Colorado's FY 2004-2005, 39.1% of youth received a new felony or misdemeanor filing prior to discharge. Post-discharge recidivism rates indicated that 37.9% of youth discharged in FY 2004-2005 received a new felony or misdemeanor filing within one year, which was consistent with a four-year trend of post-discharge recidivism rates remaining between 34.4% and 38%. Reports from FY 2009-2010 indicate 35.5% pre-discharge and 33.9% post-discharge recidivism among juvenile offenders (Research and Evaluation Unit, DYC, 2012). It is important to remember that these percentages do not include all re-offenses given that some crimes go unreported and others unsolved.

Youth who come into contact with the legal system may be subject to one or more available residential placement settings, programming methods, and individual and/or familial services at any time prior to, during, or after having been incarcerated or detained. Given the vast diversity of legal sanctions, such experiences may or may not afford overall benefits to adolescents. Commonly, the environments in which these youth typically interact on the outs remain unchanged regardless of the juvenile's contact with the legal system. That is, youth typically return to the same neighborhood, family, and peer networks. Therefore, it is conceivable that without attitudinal or behavioral changes, gained skills and strategies for navigating these settings, or access to and awareness of available resources, these adolescents will reengage with these environments in familiar or habitual ways, or ways that have otherwise proven, at least in some ways, as mechanisms for survival. For example, without gaining employment skills, an adolescent returning to his community may be unsuccessful at obtaining a job and could revert to selling drugs as a means of earning needed money. It appears that youth who are reintegrated into their original contextual settings, without the addition of new skills to navigate the impending circumstances, are in no way better prepared than when they were taken into state custody. Furthermore, the presence of new skills may not be enough in the absence of change within the community at large and the subsystems themselves. "Unfortunately, little is known about the critical components of the reentry process or the specific skills needed by incarcerated youth to make their transition from detention more successful" (Evans, Brown, & Killian, 2002, p. 554).

When comparing male recidivists with non-recidivists, Katsiyannis and Archwamety (1997) identified 11 significant differences that existed between the two (e.g., first commitment, severity of offenses, gang membership, and special education needs). Age of first commitment was eliminated on the premise that youth who were younger when first committed had greater eligibility for recommitment given that the facility served youth between the ages of 12 and 18 (i.e., a 12 year old has a greater chance of recommitment than a 17 year old). These variables were then analyzed using a logistic regression analysis. According to the results, the three variables most predictive of recidivism were age at first offense, math achievement pretest score upon first commitment, and length of stay (Katsiyannis & Archwamety). The younger a youth is when he commits his first crime increases the likeliness and opportunity for him to re-offend. As previously discussed, factors surrounding education play a significant role in the lives of youth who become involved with the juvenile justice processes. More specifically, youth who are behind in grade level or basic skills such as mathematics may experience greater difficulty in the classroom setting. As a result, it is conceivable that youth returning to their communities may be unsuccessful in school or not return to school at all, a system which has the potential to mitigate recidivism. Lastly, length of stay was found to be greater among recidivists. This may have to do with the efficacy of treatment programs being implemented or the amount of family support received during one's stay.

When youth return to their communities, it is not uncommon for them to encounter a host of challenges, enhancing their vulnerability to reengage in criminal behaviors. The following excerpt serves as an example to highlight the struggles encountered by one White youthful offender:

> After [the level 6 placement] I got my life together a little bit. I was doing good, living on my own with my girlfriend...Then we started having a lot of arguments and it was not good for the baby, and I lost my job and then she kicked me out. I was stressed out...I was awful. I started doin' drugs and feeling like I was going to explode. I imagined doing a robbery to make some money. I put on a ski mask and broke into a girl's house. (Lane, Lanza-Kaduce, Frazier, and Bishop, 2002, p. 439).

When interviewed, incarcerated youth commonly indicated that difficulties obtaining employment, proximity or availability of crime, and relational difficulties contributed to eventually giving up trying (Lane et al., 2002). For example, one Black youth shared, "I stopped selling drugs for a while but I felt like I just wasn't getting anywhere. My mom needed help, and I started slingin' again" (Lane et al., p. 439).

Qualitative interviews with formerly incarcerated adolescents revealed a series of factors that contribute to a youth's discontinuation of crime (Todis, Bullis, Waintrup, Schultz, & D'Ambrosio, 2001), including the following: active family involvement and communication; successful return and engagement in school; participation in work activities; associations with positive peers (i.e., those who abstain from illegal activity or engage in prosocial ways); refraining from substance use; and, consistent relations with at least one positive adult besides a parent. These findings are consistent with those of Masten (2001) who indicated that converging evidence substantiates the significance of a relatively small group of global factors that support effective interaction between youth and their environment, thereby enhancing their potential for success. These global factors include attachment to competent and caring adults, a positive self-view, self-regulation skills, cognitive skills, and motivation (Masten).

Researchers agree that incarcerated youth who acquire greater academic competence are less likely to re-offend and present a greater likelihood of future success (Baltodano et al., 2005; Leone & Cutting, 2004). Educational accomplishments also have the potential to increase self-confidence and attachment to school (Wang et al., 2005). Previously incarcerated youth who become actively engaged in education upon release have been found to be less likely to commit future offenses (Bullis & Yovanoff, 2005). Community adjustment has also been identified as being directly related to the first six months after release, a period within which engagement in school and/or employment appears to have a positive impact (Bullis, Yovanoff, & Havel, 2004). This body of literature suggests that previously incarcerated youth need purpose and belonging either through school or rewarding work.

In order to serve these youth effectively and efficiently it is imperative that we gain a more explicit understanding of the continual needs and difficulties faced by this population (Bullis et al., 2002). Research examining the process of reentry has historically been narrowly focused on recidivism outcomes (Spencer & Jones-Walker, 2004). More recent studies have begun to examine the reentry process by exploring the needs of subgroups of youth. In this regard, transition services specifically tailored to the needs of students with disabilities have been identified as reducing recidivism likeliness among this population (Clark, Mathur, & Helding, 2011). Also, Fields and Abrams identified differences that may contribute to "gender-specific reentry services" noting perceived needs upon reentry as well as potential barriers to success (2010). For example, while both males and females reported employment goals, young men were more likely to consider illegal options to obtain money. Also, young women presented with greater anxiety about anticipated living circumstances and reuniting with their families. Collectively, participants expressed concerns about their success upon reentry but did not anticipate utilizing community-based services as a means to support their transition (Fields & Abrams, 2010). Findings from studies such as these have the potential to begin informing the development of successful reentry programs and altering currently used transition practices.

These studies also underscore the reality that focus on recidivism outcomes alone cannot capture adequately the multitude of known interacting factors experienced by youth returning to their communities, their family systems, and their community schools. Therefore, gaining deeper insight into the daily life experiences of these adolescents through their own personal perceptions may contribute valuable new information regarding the transition of reintegration from state custody.

SUMMARY

Currently, research has identified numerous internal and external factors that play a role in the initiation, continuation, and reengagement in illegal activities among youth. When considering Bandura's (1986) triadic reciprocal determinism, the interplay among three sets of domains – namely, cognitions and personal factors, behavior, and environment – provides a framework for organizing the many variables that contribute to criminal behavior in youth. For those youth who become incarcerated, it is conceivable that some variables that lead them to become involved with illegal activities are similar to those that contribute to their reengagement in such acts upon release. Without a change in the environmental and/or intraindividual forces, it is unrealistic to expect a permanent positive change in behavior. It is important to include the voices of those youth who have lived these experiences as a contributing component to the literature about this phenomenon.

CHAPTER 3
Photovoice

A QUALITATIVE APPROACH

Qualitative research is guided by philosophical and personal assumptions, as well as interpretive and theoretical frameworks, that inform the research and writing processes. As such, Creswell (2007) stated that "good research requires making these assumptions, paradigms, and frameworks explicit...to be aware of that they influence the conduct of inquiry" (p. 15). Qualitative inquiry is characterized by the belief in multiple realities as well as enhanced understanding when research is conducted among participants for an extended period of time (Creswell). For this reason, I chose a design that encouraged participants to share their perspective using a Photovoice process.

Photovoice engages participants in the research process by providing group members with cameras to visually depict their perceptions of their lives and communities. Images are then used to guide critical discussion among group members and further, impart new knowledge to community members and policy makers. Previously incarcerated youth have firsthand knowledge about their experiences in the legal system, one that is likely unknown to researchers and the professionals who might work with them. Further, these individuals rarely have an opportunity to share meaningful insights that might influence decisions over their lives (e.g., legislation, probation and parole decisions, correctional facility rules and regulations, etc.). I believed that engagement in a Photovoice project upon returning to their communities would offer such an opportunity, allowing for these youth to counteract stereotypes and influence public perceptions concerning issues they perceived as important (Wang et al., 2000). The theoretical underpinnings of Photovoice include tenets of Freirean and Feminist theory, as well as that of documentary photography. There is a commonality among these three as they all address issues concerning persons who typically hold little, if any power, such as young adults who have been incarcerated.

Freirean Theory

Photovoice is based on the theoretical underpinnings inherent in Freire's (1970/1995/2005) approach to critical education. According to Freirean theory, individuals who encounter oppression, naturally assume the structure of domination that exists within larger society. The foundational principles expressed in *Pedagogy of the Oppressed* asserted that, despite their depth of submersion among a class of oppression, group members are in a position to identify fundamental issues that influence their lives. Therefore, youth who have the shared experience of adjudication represent a group whose possible worldview is distinct from those of mainstream society who are unable to share this view given their naivety to this experience. Freirean theory contends that critical dialogue consuming the central issues affecting their lives enables group members to recognize common themes. "With the proper tools, anyone can gradually perceive his or her personal and social reality as well as contradictions in it, become conscious of those personal perceptions, and deal critically with them" (Wang & Redwood-Jones, 2001, p. 561). Freire promoted the potential impact of the visual image as a means of representing and enabling discussion of the social and political realities of a community. In Photovoice, this concept is directly introduced and strengthened because participants choose what will be depicted in the images (Wang & Burris, 1997).

Feminism

Photovoice also reflects elements of feminist theory (Strack et al., 2004; Wang & Burris, 1997; Wang et al., 1996; Wang et al., 2000). According to Wang et al. (1996), feminist theory promotes the view that "…knowledge or practice that exploits or oppresses is unjustifiable," (p. 1392). Furthermore, "feminist theory suggests that power accrues to those who have voice, set language, make history, and participate in decisions" (Smith, 1987, as cited in Wang & Redwood-Jones, 2001, p. 561; Wang et al., 2000, p. 82). Certain voices have historically been, and in some cases continue to be, excluded from policy development and decision making that directly influences their lives. The theoretical underpinnings of Feminism contribute to Photovoice in that this reality is fully acknowledged. Furthermore, Photovoice research seeks to mitigate this problem by appreciating that everyone has a right to be heard and, moreover, proactively pursuing underrepresented groups. This Photovoice project sought to offer adolescents who have experienced incarceration an opportunity to have their concerns heard by community members and policy makers who may be influential in their lives or the lives of youth similar to them.

Documentary Photography

Documentary photography has been used frequently to enhance awareness of social issues; however, the images chosen for such illustration are often in the hands of outsiders, thereby representing an etic standpoint rather than that which is experienced by the members of the subculture(s) being represented (Strack et al., 2004, Wang & Burris, 1994, 1997; Wang et al., 1996). For example, this approach has been implemented to highlight the unfavorable conditions of working class citizens by photographing urban decline, rural poverty, and the decline of small farming communities (Rosler, 1989). While this method has great potential to enhance consciousness of social and political issues, it does not, in and of itself, create change. Photovoice takes documentary photography one step further by sharing participants' photos in purposeful ways intended to facilitate potential social activism among policy makers and community members.

Photovoice Projects

Photovoice has been used globally with a wide variety of groups with various goals in mind. It is fair to say that Photovoice projects represent a broad range of focus points with respect to the age and geographic location of participants and with regard to the public health issue at the center of each project. Studies to date include groups representing multiple ages, as well as those with exclusively youth or adult participants. Geographically, the countries represented through Photovoice research include but are not limited to Peru, Kenya, Canada, Papua New Guinea, China, and the US. Deep exploration into subcultures have looked into the lives of rural Appalachian youth, individuals living with hidden and observable disabilities and medical diagnoses, the experiences of college students, individuals living in impoverished communities, and broader-based public health issues such as HIV/AIDS and even community-felt affects related to global climate change. Increasingly, research is beginning to document the possible utility of Photovoice for proactive prevention and intervention in areas such as childhood obesity and substance use.

One of the commonalities shared among these projects has been the desire to glean information from persons who have not otherwise had the opportunity to directly influence the policies under which they live, work, or receive assistance. For example, Wang et al. (1996) implemented Photovoice with a group of Chinese village women as one component of the Ford Foundation-supported Women's Reproductive Health and Development Program in two rural counties of Yunnan province. A slide presentation of the women's photographs, presented to the Provincial and County Guidance Groups, resulted in the initiation of day care for the infants of women laborers involved with tobacco and corn farming. It also served as a catalyst for a training program for midwives given that the women expressed concerns regarding the lack of accessible medical assistance. This excerpt by one participating woman, Fu Qiong, who photographed a mother with her three-day old infant, helps to demonstrate the importance of information that may be shared through this process.

> I wanted to show the poor medical, hygiene, and health service conditions for women in the countryside. This woman did her labor at home...Rural women have very little knowledge about gynecology and reproductive health. The main reason this woman did not go to the hospital for labor was financial difficulties...If their economic situation allowed them to pay the delivery fee, all would be willing to go to the hospital because they understand it would be safer for both the mother's and the child's health...(Wang et al., p.1397).

Scholarships for young women to attend school also transpired from photos, as did discussions about changing current attitudes regarding female education (Wang et al., 1996). Strack et al. (2004) also noted ways in which youth photos were received by policy makers. For example, one 12-year-old's photo was accompanied by the caption, "My middle school is a bad school. The ceiling is falling apart and is not good" (Strack et al., p. 53). After viewing the image, one policy maker promised to investigate the situation further. Community- and policy-level outcomes vary widely across the differing projects. A Photovoice project conducted in Papua New Guinea among young adults (mean age 22) focused on their perceptions of positive and negative health influences. Insights revealed direct and indirect effects of policy on young people's behavioral choices -- and therefore potential health outcomes. When discussing educational fees (required for both primary and secondary schooling) one participant, Elsie, shared:

> When I am in the school I didn't smoke or drink but when my parents didn't pay my school fees I am very

angry with them. When I am angry with my parents I am
smoking drugs and drinking alcohol and whatever other
things I want to do (Vaughan, 2010, p. 1648).

Although meaningful influences to health behaviors were
identified, reception by local policy makers differed between the
two groups that participated. Vaughan suggested that resulting
local action was influenced by pre-existing community variables
such as cohesiveness and the support of nearby leadership
highlighting that, in such situations, finding ways to engage
influential adults may be equally, if not more valuable (Vaughan,
2010).

In addition to educating policy makers and increasing voice
among marginalized populations, Photovoice has provided
participants, oftentimes group members of subcultures lacking
power, with a means by which to counter stereotypes often
imposed on them by outside observers. As previously discussed
in Chapter 1, this was the case with the *Language of Light*
Photovoice project. Participants of this project were utilizing
homeless shelters and expressed the desire to impart knowledge
about the everyday struggles encountered by persons
experiencing homelessness (Wang et al., 2000). One participant
in particular educated policy makers about the fact that although
persons may be living in a shelter, they may be working or
seeking employment.

Participation in Photovoice projects can be especially
empowering for participants (Wang & Burris, 1997). In the
Language of Light Photovoice project, one 18-year-old female
participant explained, "I was busy, and that was such a
wonderful feeling; and my feeling of esteem went way up"
(Wang et al., 2000, p. 86). Strack et al. (2004) also described a
similar outcome with the adolescent participants in their
Photovoice project. They explained, "...the youth's own photos
created a great sense of pride and ownership that contributed to
their exchange of views. This newfound strength seemed to
embolden the youth with a degree of authority and zeal when
describing their photographs..." (Strack et al., p. 52).

Furthermore, they noted that youth experienced feelings of empowerment as evidenced by gained insights about community strengths and weaknesses, feelings of recognition and pride associated with sharing photos at exhibits, and increased thoughts about their communities and the roles they play within them (Strack et al.).

Recently, Photovoice has been employed as a means of informing proactive prevention and intervention efforts. A project was completed in Western Kenya, with adolescents (ages 12 through 17) from rural communities who shared the all too common experience there of caring for parent(s) with AIDS. Guiding questions focused on the identification of coping strategies among participants which were later used to inform the development and implementation of action plans intended strengthen these coping mechanisms (Skovdal, 2011). Photovoice research was similarly used as one component of community assessment completed by Union County Fit Kids, a program focusing research efforts on the prevention of childhood obesity in Oregon. They involved six adolescents (ages 15 through 18) to identify noteworthy community barriers and assets regarding food choices and engagement in physical activity among children (Findholt, Michael, & Davis, 2011). The group members identified several benefits of their participation, including learning about the factors that influence children's health, and more individually-based benefits such as overcoming shyness and future plans to pursue a career in a health field. While the information gathered was intended to inform the development of targeted interventions, small changes among the participants themselves appear to also be positive and potentially influential with regard to childhood obesity. Individual meaning for participants of Photovoice projects seems to bear equal value to the outcomes associated with community awareness and change. One group member of a Photovoice project representing individuals who were living with brain injury, "...said that her family members read the poster and project booklet. She felt, for perhaps the first time in the 31 years since her accident, that they had shown interest in and respect for something she had done"

(Lorenz, 2010, p. 219). Overall, research conducted using Photovoice seems to result in positive outcomes among participants in most instances and oftentimes occasions improvements in their surrounding communities.

ROLE OF THE RESEARCHERS

Qualitative inquiry presumes that all researchers hold certain values that may influence decisions throughout the research process (Creswell, 2007). One way to strengthen the trustworthiness of findings is to explicitly disclose this information at the outset, thereby allowing the reader to interpret the study in light of this information. Therefore, in the following section, my research assistant and I have described our previous experience and knowledge as it related at the time of the study.

Principal Investigator

Children and adolescents are all too often confronted with adverse experiences, at times leading to behavioral choices that similarly result in negative outcomes. Adolescents are faced with such challenges as unplanned pregnancy, attempted and actual suicide among peers and relatives, family discord, drug addiction and overdose, and personal and family involvement with the justice system. As a teenager, I witnessed first-hand these unfavorable life circumstances affecting young adults around me. In retrospect, I realized that many of these individuals and peer groups repeated the cycle of bullying and chose to handle problems using maladaptive coping strategies. Oftentimes, young people like this are stereotyped or targeted as problems in the school setting, a place that could otherwise serve to strengthen their resilience and mitigate the hardships they encounter elsewhere. This reality contributed to my research interests with youth from a variety of cultural backgrounds, specifically focused on prevention and intervention of emotional and behavioral disorders, and the relationship between poor academic achievement or negative educational experiences and subsequent antisocial outcomes. Unfortunately, youth of color and individuals with mental health and learning disorders are overrepresented in juvenile corrections settings and many of these young people have been affected by experiences that do not support optimal development. I believe that the external behaviors that result in incarceration are the product of a host of biological, social, psychological, and environmental factors that include the experience of victimization, as well as being blamed and repeatedly ostracized by systems that are theoretically in place to mitigate these exact issues. We may consider the development of innovative programs and continued research as valiant efforts to make changes for this group; however, this does not negate the many ways they continue to be underserved. We need to find effective ways to intervene and create the possibility for better outcomes so that all youth have a chance to reach their fullest potential.

Associate Investigator

Kristin L. Johnson-Schrader, who was completing the requirements for a doctoral degree in school psychology at the time of the project, assumed the role of research assistant. Kristin provided the following description of her involvement and interest in the phenomena of youth crime.

I have worked very closely and built relationships with children who have experienced more pain in their short lives than I could ever imagine possible. There is often a sense of hopelessness, of powerlessness, and of hurt so deep that one wonders how they will ever come out of it. Their families are disintegrating, their communities are failing to provide support, and they seemingly have nowhere to go but down. Yet some of them survive. Why is that? My interest in working with previously incarcerated youth has to do with the outcomes. What factors help them spiral down? What factors help lift them up? What are their perceptions of these factors? How do we prevent and intervene with these youth on a community-wide basis to promote successful outcomes and help raise healthy adults? These youth have a voice that we are not listening to, one that can give us valuable insight into how to effectively impact and prevent such a negative cycle.

FUNDING

This study was partially supported by monetary contributions and donations gifted by local businesses, and friends and family[1]. Additionally, I was awarded a $500 grant by the Graduate Student Association of the University of Northern Colorado for costs associated with my research.

PROCEDURES

Before beginning the project and throughout its completion, I consulted with various individuals to assist with the planning, implementation, and analysis of the project. When determining specific components of the methodology (e.g., participant selection, curriculum development), I consulted with a licensed psychologist who was employed at a state facility serving detained and committed adolescents. He shared suggestions regarding participant recruitment, safety (i.e., home visits, involving family, gang concerns, etc.), and the weekly meetings. More specifically, he reviewed tentative outlines for weekly meetings and provided feedback for strengthening the plans. For example, he recommended reducing the project duration from 20 sessions, as initially intended, to a shorter, more manageable time frame. He noted the potential challenges associated with maintaining prolonged voluntary involvement on the part of any

[1] David Dougherty and *Epic Images*; Ryan Dougherty; Aric Hanisch; One Hour Photo Express; County Assessor's Office; Cesar Chavez Cultural Center; Solecki Chiropractic; Classic Lanes; Highland Park Lanes; Qdoba; Cinemark; (continued on next page…)
Salvador Deli; Chipotle; Palomino Mexican Restaurant; Island Grille; Buffalo Wild Wings; King Soopers; Papa John's; Cold Stone; Family Fun Plex; Hunan Imperial; Bissett Nursery in Holtsville, NY

individual but emphasized that the stressors and risks that contribute to attrition are greater among this population (e.g., high mobility, recidivism). Therefore the project length was limited to a more realistic time-frame that would increase the chances that group members would be available each week and successfully complete the project. I additionally consulted with a licensed psychologist who facilitated the implementation of a large scale Photovoice project among children and families with mental health needs, the *Wyoming SAGE* Photovoice project (*Wyoming Photovoice*). He provided suggestions regarding the development of the Photovoice curriculum, implementation of Photovoice sessions, and preparation and execution of the exhibit. Two senior researchers were also consulted for their expertise in qualitative research and Photovoice studies.

Participants

Participant recruitment. Strack et al. (2004) recommended a youth-to-adult ratio of 5:1 or less when conducting Photovoice research with youth participants. Given the heightened potential for attrition among this population of youth, I originally sought to start with seven male participants. The decision to develop a homogeneous gender sample was threefold: (a) males are disproportionately represented in juvenile correctional facilities; (b) males and females have traditionally tended to become incarcerated for distinctly different offenses; and, (c) including one to two females would run the risk of losing female voice among a group dominated by male participants.

In qualitative research, sample selection is generally non-random, purposeful, and involves small numbers of cases (Merriam, 1998). To identify participants, we contacted local service-providers working with youth identified as "at-risk" or involved with the legal system. We explained the nature of the project and asked that they subsequently discuss it with adolescents believed to be good candidates (e.g., willing to work with rival gang members, expressed willingness or desire to change, available for weekly meetings, etc.).

Through this process I received a call from a local parole officer interested in referring some of his parolees for the study. At the time, these young men were all participating in a weekly art therapy group that he facilitated with a therapist. I made arrangements and visited this group on two successive occasions. During those visits I explained the project and each of the young men present expressed an interest in participating. I also received three additional referrals, two of which came from another parole officer. The remaining referral was made by the director of a local non-profit organization serving young adults. I gathered contact information for these potential participants and arranged to meet with each of them to explain the project and to acquire informed consent/assent.

Consent was obtained from five of the seven young men (or their parents when needed). Of the five youth in question one young man withdrew the morning of the first meeting because of safety concerns related to gang activity. He explained that he had decided to end involvement with his previous gang associates. After witnessing a gang-related fight and choosing not to partake, he anticipated being the victim of retaliation in the form of physical violence by the members of his previous gang, some of whom at the time had agreed to participate in the group.

Of the remaining four young men expected, three arrived the first evening. I felt it was important to begin the group as scheduled with those who showed up. I also believed that continuing to recruit new members after having begun the group would create challenges given the cumulative nature of the curriculum and the emphasis on building relationships. Consequently, I made the decision to proceed. Because of information provided by his parole officer, and acquaintances in the group, the potential fourth member was not contacted – nor did he attempt to contact us.

Group members. Weekly groups were attended by three male participants, each whom had recently returned to his community from a secure placement in state's custody on account of illegal behavior. The members were either 17- or 18-years-old. Two young men identified themselves as Mexican, or

Mexican-American, and one as Caucasian. All of the participants were on parole at the time of the study.

Setting

The data for this study were collected in Colorado during the fall of 2008. Our weekly meetings were held at a local facility owned and operated by a non-profit organization whose mission is to serve the spiritual needs of young people through a variety of weekly activities, regular events, and partnerships with nearby churches and businesses. They provided us access to their building and use of their technology resources. This facility was chosen because of its central location and proximity to the local bus route (for participants who may have needed transportation). At the time of the study, the interior was designed and decorated to be adolescent-friendly and the building was used for many prosocial activities such as sports and games. Moreover, it offered a way to acquaint the group members with a positive community resource beyond simply a meeting space for our groups. The physical structure allowed us to meet privately, and the technology available made it possible to play video clips and depict the participants' images on a large screen for the group to view simultaneously.

Facilitators

Weekly sessions were facilitated by me, and co-facilitated by my research assistant, Kristin, and David Dougherty, a professional photographer and owner of *Epic Images*. Together we engaged in weekly meetings by each participating actively in ice breakers, asking questions of the participants during photo discussions, and informal interactions. Individual roles differed in that I played a leadership role in designing and administrating weekly sessions and executing the various stages of the research process, while Kristin's role involved assisting with the research elements of the sessions, and David supported the photographic aspects of the project. At meetings, Kristin recorded detailed notes that included observations (e.g., arrival time, displayed emotion), record of participants' descriptions of photographs and group discussion, and her own personal comments and perceptions of the sessions as a whole or individual participants. The photographic components that David guided included educating participants about photography (i.e., camera functions, photography techniques, and artistic organization), familiarizing group members with various types of images, and leading a photo expedition. Given David's expertise in photography, his role was focused primarily in this area and was less involved in the research centered aspects of the project.

Weekly Meetings

This Photovoice project was conducted over a period of eight consecutive weeks. For the first seven sessions, the group met for approximately two hours. At the conclusion, all members attended a four-hour photo exhibit where their work was displayed. An informal meeting was held prior to the gallery and a celebratory dinner was held afterwards. This project was originally designed to follow a series of consecutive stages, guided by the suggested elements to be included in Photovoice projects (Wang, 2005), and a timeline and curriculum guide that Strack et al. (2004) suggested for carrying out Photovoice with exclusively youth participants. Consistent with general Photovoice procedure, the sessions occurred in a successive manner, youth participants were educated about the project and photography, they engaged in critical dialogue surrounding pictures, and shared the overall findings with community members and policy makers. The number of sessions, however, was reduced to reflect the suggestions made during consultation. Given the emergent nature of the study, the curriculum was additionally modified as deemed appropriate while in progress. Table 1 describes the weekly activities as they were implemented.

The activities for each session were generally pre-determined and adjustments were made to reflect the changing needs of the participants, time restrictions, and unanticipated events. A meal was provided at the start of each session.

Icebreakers were also incorporated at the beginning of each meeting to build relationships, develop leadership and team-building skills, and initiate meetings with a fun, positive task. The chosen icebreakers required increasingly greater levels of self-disclosure and provided opportunities to practice skills relevant to the overall project goals (e.g., telling stories, thinking about goals post-incarceration, etc.). Participants received weekly incentives for their attendance and participation. Incentives were chosen based on participant interest, involvement in positive community activities, or for the purpose of increasing prosocial skills and talents among group members (e.g., books, gift certificates, art supplies). After successfully completing the project by attending the gallery, each group member was additionally able to keep his digital camera and given a scrapbook containing his photographs.

One of the main goals of our weekly meetings was to help participating group members to understand the nature of Photovoice and comprehend the purpose of the study. In addition to discussing these components with the young men, group activities were specifically selected to develop this awareness. For example, as a group, we explored websites centered on Photovoice and viewed completed Photovoice projects (i.e., published articles, projects publicized on websites, and images, titles, and captions created by young people involved in a Photovoice study). Furthermore, the *Wyoming SAGE* Photovoice project identifies several roles (i.e., Social Activists, Storytellers, Researchers, Leaders) assumed by members of a Photovoice project (*Wyoming Photovoice*). The lessons were designed to help group members begin to consider these roles, practice the skills inherent in these functions, and explore how others have adopted these responsibilities. Lastly, elements of photography (i.e., teaching photography techniques, familiarizing participants with various types of images, practicing, discussing personal images) were incorporated into every meeting.

The first two sessions were focused on developing group cohesiveness, building awareness of photography and photo ethics, and preparing group members to consider the strengths and issues of their communities. The majority of time spent during later group meetings centered on viewing and discussing participants' photographs. Toward the end of the project, group activities were concentrated on exhibit arrangements.

The following section describes the execution of each of the aspects of Photovoice, and how these processes were incorporated into this study. The format is modeled after the presentation used by Strack et al. (2004). Furthermore, it is closely aligned with Wang and Burris' (1997) method for involving participants in analysis. They outlined this three-stage process (i.e., selecting, contextualizing or storytelling, and codifying) when describing the application of Photovoice to participatory needs assessments in public health research.

IMPLEMENTING THE THREE COMPONENTS OF PHOTOVOICE

Taking Pictures

For the purposes of this project, participating members were asked to take photographs throughout the week between one meeting to the next. For the initial two weeks, participating youth were each provided with a disposable camera. After successfully shooting all of the film and returning these cameras, they were given digital cameras to use for the remainder of the project. As a group, members were instructed on the use of both types of cameras upon receipt, and additionally as needed. On average, disposable film cameras and digital media allowed for about 16-24 color images to be taken weekly. The number of actual photos varied weekly for each participant. A number of factors contributed to these differences. For example, one young man reported frequently forgetting his camera at home, thereby limiting the number of images he returned; at times, a participant would request a few additional days to finish taking all of the images; one participant asked for another memory card in order to take more photos each week.

Prior to distributing cameras, photo ethics were discussed with the participants. Initial ethics instruction focused on safety issues and emphasized that personal safety should supersede taking any images that might place themselves or others in harm. During the first two weeks, group members were asked to take images of places and things, specifically excluding people. They were given business cards to distribute should anyone inquire about them taking photos or how the photos would be used. During the third meeting, each of the group members was additionally provided with several copies of a Photo Consent form which we discussed as a group. This document was intended to explain the project and obtain permission from persons who may be photographed.

Initially, I used broad directives to instigate photo-taking throughout the following week. For example, youth were instructed to "take pictures of things that impact your life." What seemed to work better was posing a question or asking the group members to consider a specific aspect of their lives and brainstorming the types of things they might photograph to show those. For example, the participants were asked to list some of their personal strengths and weaknesses. They were able to consider that in group, list some ideas, and then return with photos depicting these or similar components of their lives in addition to photos taken spontaneously.

After taking a week's worth of film, all images were developed digitally – i.e., electronic copies were used in lieu of traditionally printed photos. Participants then met individually with David, during which time they viewed their photos and chose three images to share during that evening's meeting. Wang and Burris (1997) described this piece of participatory analysis as selecting, or involving participants in the process of choosing the photos that best represent community strengths and needs. The photos were then projected onto a large screen, allowing the group to simultaneously view individual photos as they were discussed.

Table 1. Photovoice Weekly Curriculum

Topic/Session	Activities
Introduction to Photovoice	
Session 1	Welcome: introductions, confidentiality, establishing group norms Introduction to Photovoice Exposure to photographs Photo ethics Introduction to disposable cameras/photography Video Clip of a photo exhibit
Principles of Photography	
Session 2	Photograph discussion Get youth thinking about their community and themselves as researchers Video Clips of adolescents sharing stories, and engaging in social activism Photo ethics Photography instruction
Discussion of Photographs	
Session 3	Photograph discussion Introduction to digital cameras/photography Photo expedition Introduction of the SHOWeD Method Viewed examples of titles and captions in other Photovoice projects Writing captions and titles
Session 4	Photograph discussion
Session 5	Photograph discussion Get youth thinking about their community and themselves as researchers
Session 6	Photograph discussion
Exhibit Preparation	
Session 7	Caption and title writing Formal member check of photo groupings
Session 8	Formal member check of biographies Visit to gallery facility Discussion about gallery
Session 9	Photo Exhibit

Group Discussion of Photos

When sharing photos, we generally used the following routine: images were shared in three rotations, during which each member shared one image. This strategy was chosen to keep group members engaged, ensure that all attending members were given ample time to discuss their images, and to avoid having discussion focused only on one member's photos. Each image was depicted on a large screen for all to see while the photographer spoke about his image. Telling the meaning of photos, or contextualizing, is considered by Wang and Burris (1997) as another aspect of participatory analysis. In this study, initial participant descriptions often included comments such as why the photographer took the picture, what he liked about it, and where he was when it was taken. Group members were subsequently encouraged to ask questions and offer comments. Facilitated group discussion was intertwined with this process. The participants were consulted about and agreed to digitally record weekly meetings which were later transcribed and reviewed. Lastly, David commented on the artistic elements of the images, noting strengths and providing constructive feedback for ways to continue improving photography skills.

Initially, I planned to use the SHOWeD method of critical dialoging to facilitate the discussion of participants' photos (Strack et al., 2004; Wang et al., 2000). This method has commonly been used in previous Photovoice studies. It follows a standard set of questions for discussing the meaning depicted in participants' images.

S What do you See here?
H What is really Happening?
O How does there relate Our lives?
W Why does this problem or strength exist?
e
D What can we Do about it?

In general, the participants in this study had difficulty answering these questions about their photos. Similar difficulties have been noted in Photovoice studies with youth participants. For example, Wilson et al. (2007) indicated that youth (ages 9 through 12) had difficulty formulating analytical responses using the SHOWeD method to guide freewrites about their images. Furthermore, Strack et al. (2004) noted the initial tendency of youth participants (ages 11 through 17) toward taking pictures of things of interest to them and using the images, "...as a way to tell the world about themselves" (Strack et al., p. 52). This was similarly true among our group members. Many of their photos depicted interests, likes, and ways they identified themselves. Photos also represented their attempts to experiment with photography techniques or capture images of artistic quality. Participants did not find the questions used in the SHOWeD method applicable to many of these types of photographs. From their perspective, the pictures clearly depicted what was happening in the image; they had difficulty moving to a more abstract level of analysis. For example, one participant described his photo by saying, "Yeah, that is my girlfriend. I took a picture of her close up. I think it looks good. I like it." Questions such as "What is really Happening?" seemed confusing in instances such as these because of the concrete fashion in which the participant had introduced and perceived his photo.

Adapting the SHOWeD method by asking open-ended questions that were directly related to an individual's photo allowed participant-generated images to be used as a foundation for further exploration and discussion of community strengths and weaknesses. The participants easily answered posed questions that were more focused such as "Tell us more about your relationship" and "How does the fact that the teacher yells at you impact your experience at school?" This led to further exploration because I was able to encourage input from other group members and facilitate the discussion between them. For example, in one instance a photo of a plant led to a discussion about the participants' experiences with and perceptions of teachers, information which lends itself to the underlying purpose of Photovoice regarding identifying the role of community assets and needs in their lives.

Caption and Title Development

One of the goals of the project was to place the participants in a
position to influence the direction and outcome of the study as
often as possible. They chose which images to share with the
group each week and developed the title and caption to
accompany each photo. Similar to photo discussion, participant-
generated captions are additionally considered by Wang and
Burris (1997) as a form of contextualizing, a participatory
analysis strategy employed with Photovoice.

I had originally planned to include time each week for
creating these; however, I quickly realized that this was a less
efficient use of time. For one, participant-generated captions
were very similar to their initial description given during group.
Furthermore, participants needed a significant amount of time to
formulate their descriptors. At first they seemed to perceive that
there was a "right" and "wrong" response. As a result, we spent a
great deal of time and the end product was not much different
from the group explanation, making the process overly
repetitive. Moreover, transcribed sessions allowed us to access
the initial descriptors, which felt upon reflection to be more
genuine and informal. I decided instead to focus more time on
sharing and discussing participant photos, and consequently
dedicated Session 7 to the development of titles and captions.

During that session, the group members were provided with
printed copies of each of their photographs, as well as paper and
pen for participant note-taking. Kristin and I met with each
participant who dictated the title and caption for one or two
images at a time. We rotated among the group members,
indicating which image they should prepare to talk about next.
This allowed participants to focus on creating their descriptions
without taking away from other activities. We also used the
transcriptions to remind members of what they had initially
shared with the group when discussing a particular image.

When assisting the participants to develop their captions,
Kristin and I sought to maximize their independence and control.
The participants verbally dictated their captions, which Kristin
and I recorded to prevent any barriers that might exist due to

literacy skills. Because the participants had already shared the details of individual images, it seemed that they sometimes forgot that others viewing their photos would not be similarly aware of this information. A few times we sought clarification and used prompting questions to help the participants refine their captions to best express their intended meaning. For example, on one occasion we asked the participant to consider what he wanted others to know about his experience. By answering that question, he was able to formulate a caption that focused on the precise story he wanted to tell.

The titles and captions were translated into Spanish and they were posted in both English and Spanish at the gallery. Due to time restrictions, all project documents could not be translated. Because the captions represented the voice of participating members, I chose to have those translated so that English and Spanish-speaking gallery attendees could read them in their primary language.

Informing Policy Makers: *Life on the Outs* Photovoice Gallery

Biographies. Biographies were created for each participating member as a means of introducing them to gallery attendees as both artists and researchers. Kristin and I attempted to include similar information about each of the group members (e.g., age, interests, previous photography experience) that we felt characterized them based on our interactions over the course of the project. The young men then read the biographies we had created, decided whether or not changes needed to be made, and approved them to be displayed at the gallery.

Photo grouping. The original data analysis procedures proposed to use participant codifying, the third stage of participatory analysis, according to Wang and Burris (1997). This includes the identification of "issues, themes or theories" as they emerge from group discussions (Wang & Burris, p. 381). I had originally planned to consider these weekly; however, clear dimensions of this nature did not readily appear on a weekly basis and the group members struggled to see commonalities or issues they believed could be changed.

Therefore, when deciding how to group the images for the gallery presentation, Kristin and I worked together with all images that had been taken, focusing on the meaning provided through the accompanying captions and our interactions with the participants. I first arranged the photos into clusters, discretely recording my reasoning. Next, Kristin rearranged the photos into her own perceived groupings, similarly taking undisclosed notes. Afterwards, we discussed our rationale, negotiated the placement of photos, and formed prospective groups. These groups were given temporary labels and descriptions. We then shared the proposed organization with the participants for feedback. They seemed surprised by the fact that certain photos related with others and fit into groupings and they excitedly agreed with the logic and manner in which we had grouped the photos without offering further suggestions. The group members worked together to develop titles for each of the sections. After the member-check, Kristin and I rewrote the descriptions in a bit more formal manner. The titles accompanied these formal introductions to each of the photo groups presented at the gallery.

I acknowledged that it was important for people attending the gallery to be provided with accurate information about youth incarceration and the young men in this study in order to prevent the perpetuation of stereotypes and inaccurate assumptions. We had learned a great deal about the participants as a result of spending time with them weekly and being present during their group discussions, and I felt that some of this information may not be explicitly communicated in their images alone. Therefore, introductions were developed to help attendees see the connection among photos within a specific group, and to supplement the images with supporting information.

To allow for some confidentiality, the photo groups purposely included a mixture of images from each of the participants and excluded the photographer's name. Furthermore, the participants agreed to only identify their own images when speaking with gallery attendees and excluding their names allowed them some control to choose which images they identified as their own.

Exhibits. The formal *Life on the Outs* Photovoice Gallery was held at the Cesar Chavez Cultural Center, a campus resource at the University of Northern Colorado whose mission it is to support the academic and social success of Latino/Hispanic students attending college. The initial event lasted four hours, the first of which was dedicated solely to those invited by the group members, making this a private and special time for them. As a group, we discussed who would be appropriate to invite. The participants identified friends and family, staff members with whom they had developed relationships while incarcerated, and their current parole officers. Additionally, we identified members of the academic community believed to be positive role models and who would be interested in and supportive of the participants' work as well as our own friends and family members.

A formal invitation was created and distributed to inform these persons of the exhibit. As a group, we brainstormed ideas for including an image on the invitation. The group decided to use the image depicted in Figure 1, a symbolic representation in which cameras replaced handcuffs.

Prior to printing the final copies for distribution, the draft was shared with the group members for feedback. They did not suggest any changes and indicated that a Spanish version would be unnecessary. They expressed the view that they were happy with the final product and described it as "tight," a slang term referring to something that looks good or is stylish or cool. Participants were provided with invitations for distribution and an electronic version of the invitation was also used by the facilitators to communicate information about the event to the campus community.

Attendees were able to walk throughout the room viewing the photos; several met individually with the participants who guided them through the gallery, pointing out the images they had taken and answering questions. This process worked very well to include all participants who seemed to feel more comfortable in one-on-one interactions; it provided a great opportunity for them to show off their work and receive positive feedback. See Figure 43 for a visual depiction of the exhibit.

Figure 1. Life on the Outs Photovoice Gallery – Invitation Image.

After the initial four-hour exhibit, the gallery remained accessible to the public for one week. Notification was sent electronically to the college community and was subsequently printed in the local newspaper. I was contacted by the local newspaper which invited our group to be interviewed for the story, and I was invited to speak to a graduate level qualitative research class about the project. We met at the cultural center where they were able to view the gallery. One of the participants also joined us, sharing his own experiences and answering questions posed by the reporter and class members. The gallery was also relocated to the facility where our weekly meetings had been held. The location and hours were also advertised in the local newspaper. It remained accessible for one week, during which time interested attendees could independently view the exhibit and record comments. This second site was chosen because of its immediate access by young people as well as the local church community. Although no formal data were collected regarding attendance, staff members reported that several young adults and community members who regularly access the facility observed the presentation.

TRUSTWORTHINESS

Creswell (2009) recommended the use of multiple validity strategies to determine the accuracy of findings in qualitative research. One of these strategies involved "prolonged engagement and persistent observation in the field..." (Creswell, 2007, p. 207). Given the nature of my research, I was actively involved throughout the entire process, as was my research assistant and the group members. Not only did this provide a significant amount of time spent getting to know and understand the participants, it allowed for continual member checking and peer debriefing.

Member checking is a validation strategy in which the researcher verifies his or her findings and/or interpretations with the participants (Creswell, 2009). Photovoice relies on participant-generated data (i.e., photos, captions, stories) in contrast to pure outsider interpretation. Because of this heightened level of participant involvement, informal member checking was inherent throughout the process. In addition, the descriptive biographies used to introduce the young men at the gallery, as well as the descriptions preceding each of the photo groupings, were discussed with the group members for feedback. They also played a part in creating the titles to accompany each of the photo groups.

Peer debriefing or review involves numerous conversations about the study and research process with colleagues and others in the field (Bailey, 2007). An external review of the research is also provided through conducting a peer review (Merriam, 1998). Peer reviews were conducted throughout the entire length of the research. Throughout the project, Kristin recorded detailed notes during our meetings. In addition, I kept a weekly journal documenting my perception of the sessions. Weekly she and I met to discuss the project and review our notes, clarifying any inconsistencies. After the completion of the project, Kristin additionally read the descriptions of participants and group activities for accuracy. Having been a part of the weekly meetings, she had immediate insight into these components. In addition to discussions between myself and my research assistant, I spent time consulting with other researchers regarding the interpretation and presentation of findings. The latter of the two also contributed to numerous expert reviews that involved "seeking input from someone familiar with the research topic" (Bailey, p. 118). In this regard, I worked closely with a senior researcher, two scholars familiar with qualitative inquiry, and two psychologists with whom I consulted regarding the development of the study. The licensed psychologist working in youth corrections reviewed the photo groupings, after which we discussed his view of the photos representing either risk or protective factors in the lives of the participants. This conversation contributed to further consideration on my part that has been addressed in Chapter 4 and integrated into my discussion set forth in Chapter 5.

CHAPTER 4

Youth Voice: Perspectives on Juvenile Incarceration

PART I: *LIFE ON THE OUTS* PHOTOVOICE FINDINGS

Photovoice is a methodology that seeks to bring to light the perceptions of participants by providing an opportunity for their voice to be heard. It replaces traditional communication modalities (e.g., written language, verbal expression) with photographs, allowing the images to speak for persons who may not otherwise have the literacy or language skills to express their unique experiences of reality. This project sought to offer young men who had recently reentered their communities from a custodial juvenile justice setting an opportunity to share their ideas and beliefs about the world in which they interact and highlight the aspects that they identified as important.

Please note that the names and any other identifying information have been replaced with pseudonyms to maximize confidentiality. Furthermore, one of the purposes of this research was to learn about who these young men are; therefore, I have purposely chosen to exclude explicit details regarding the offenses which resulted in their adjudication. According to the Photovoice methodology, the findings represent the collective voice of the group members rather than an outsider's independent interpretation of their lives and experiences.

In order to maintain the philosophical underpinnings of Photovoice, I have purposely tried to exclude my own interpretation here in Part I. Instead, the majority of this piece focuses on the findings as defined by the participants. Therefore, this section provides the findings in their purest possible form. It includes the photos chosen by participants to be publicly displayed at the *Life on the Outs* Photovoice Gallery and the titles and captions that they created to accompany the images. It also includes the titles and introductions used to preface each of the photo groupings and the biographies that were posted to introduce the group members at the gallery.

Biographies

The following biographies were displayed at the gallery in order to introduce the photographers to gallery attendees (please see Chapter 3 for a more thorough description of the Photovoice facilitators as well as preparation for and holding the exhibit). The biographies provide a general overview of each group member meant to supplement their photographs and offer a brief background about the young men, similar to those found in published Photovoice projects. Kristin and I drafted the biographies and subsequently shared them with each of the group members for feedback. Their comments are reflected in the final biographies, which were approved by each participant prior to display.

Marcus. Marcus is 18 years of age and has been working part-time when possible. He earned his GED while he was incarcerated and has been actively pursuing employment but noted that he has encountered great challenges. He shared that he likes rock music, riding his bike, reading, and drawing. Prior to this project, he reported never having used a digital camera and he has grown significantly in his photo-taking abilities. He took risks to incorporate new photography techniques that he learned. He has expressed an interest in further pursuing photography through classes. Marcus mentioned that one of the things that was most difficult about being incarcerated was missing his sister's birthday. Marcus is currently still on parole and has been out of custody for approximately one year.

Raul. Raul is 17 years of age and currently attends an alternative high school. He has expressed an interest in becoming a tattoo artist in the future. His photos have been insightful and reflective of who he is and his experiences related to being incarcerated. He has also opened up about his experiences while in confinement, sharing that being locked up was a positive experience for him in some aspects of his life. Raul identifies drugs, particularly methamphetamines, as contributing greatly to his choices and behaviors for which he was locked up. Incarceration helped him to get sober, and he hopes to continue to refrain from using illegal substances. While locked up he also learned how to draw and enjoyed the art therapy group he attended. He was vocal about the staff he encountered at his placements. He explained that some staff cared about him, whereas others overused their power and acted like bullies. Raul spends a lot of time watching his preschool-age brother while his mother is at work. Although he likes that this has bettered his relationship with his brother, it is also a large responsibility that often keeps him home. He has been out of custody for four months and is currently still on parole.

Eduardo. Eduardo is 18 years of age and currently attends a public high school. He has mentioned that religion plays a role in his life, his girlfriend is a huge support for him, and he loves Wu-Tang Clan and Bob Marley; he is even growing his hair into dreads. He recognized school as a positive aspect of his life. He indicated that he has really enjoyed becoming a photographer and learning how to take pictures. He was enthusiastic about taking photos and showing them to the group. His photography skills continually progressed throughout the process. He recognized that being locked up was a positive experience for him in some respects, sharing that he was able to complete several school credits and stay healthy by running. He identified his family as a strong component of his support system, and shared that he missed them and his home while incarcerated. He was especially disappointed when he was unable to spend the holidays with his family or even visit with them on Christmas. He has been out of confinement for approximately four months and is currently on parole.

Photo Groups

As noted in Chapter 3, group members generally chose three photos to share with the group each week. In order to maximize the quantity of images displayed, the majority of these images were included at the exhibit. The participants had the option to exclude any images from being shared. One image was excluded for confidentiality reasons because it depicted a tattoo that clearly revealed the last name of a participant's family member. The grouping titled *Developing Our Creative Talents* included approximately 14 additional images that were not discussed in detail during meetings but were nonetheless chosen by one or more group members to be shown. These were displayed at the gallery without titles or captions.

Each of the next sections begins with the group title created by the participants and the introduction approved by the members, followed by the photos with accompanying titles and captions that made-up the grouping. Photos depicting people or other identifying information have been blurred in an effort to maximize confidentiality. Please note that the original images were taken and displayed in color; however, they have been reproduced in black and white in this volume.[2]

Everyday Struggle. Each of the group members has indicated that they are trying to make positive changes in their lives. Similar to the ways in which they have each identified positive and negative aspects of incarceration, they have each experienced difficulties in their communities. The fact that they have been locked up can impede their attempts to change, thereby creating roadblocks on top of those they have already experienced.

The group members have described how their lives involve a lot of push and pull. For example, one group member has shown significant independent effort to obtain employment; however, that process has been very challenging. Another identifies school

---

[2] Color versions of the images can be viewed at photovoiceontheouts.wordpress.com.

as a support, but is encountering difficulties in one class that have resulted in truancy. Another group member has decided to refrain from drug use, but his previous peer group members may not be making that same choice.

Figure 2. Out But In. This picture reminds me of being locked up because sometimes I feel like I still am. I'm always at my house doing nothing, being bored – I'm taking care of my baby brother.

Figure 3. My Past & Present. Both of these things represent me. This is my past, my old lifestyle. The blue rag represents a lot of people and violence and is what I used to do. I also used to smoke more than I do now.

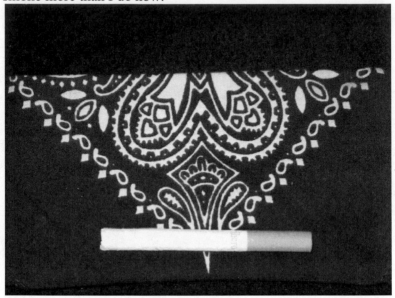

Figure 4. Easlos. This is a park where me and the homies always hang out. Most of the time there's always cops around there. That's where I first tried weed.

Figure 5. Getting Jobs. It was always hard for me to get a job after getting in trouble. Not many people want to hire someone who's been in trouble with the law but I was finally able to get a job in a kitchen.

Strengths and Weaknesses of Our Community. The photos in this section represent the strengths and weaknesses that the group members identified within their communities.

Although there are few pictures that depict racial profiling and stereotyping, this was a frequent topic of discussion and one that all members spoke about. As a group, they agreed and acknowledged that the local police tend to treat the East and West sides of town differently. More specifically, group members explained that the "cops" tend to be more predominantly on the East side of town and that they treat ethnic minorities differently. There was also some discussion of perceived misuse of power by the "cops" and race playing a role in court decision making.

Figure 6. Good and Bad. This picture represents strengths by people keeping themselves busy by working on cars and doing shows and weaknesses by if a cop sees you in this car, they are more quick to check on you than in a normal car.

Figure 7. The Castle. This is my school. I love school. One of these days I want to get my diploma so that I can go to college. I chose this picture of school because the colors are nice and I like the picture.

Figure 8. The House. It's just a messed up house, a crack house. It's on the East side where I live – in my community. It looks bad in my community. Someone should fix it up.

Figure 9. Old Firefighters. I took this picture for two reasons – because it was not too far from where I used to live, and in remembrance of those who went to New York on 9/11.

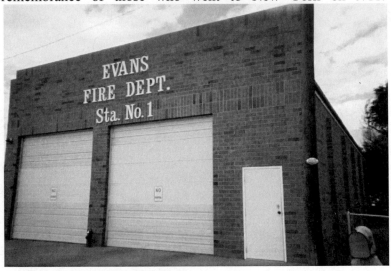

Figure 10. The School Speed Limit. This picture was taken because of all the people who do speed in an area with a school nearby. Also, to help raise awareness of things that are important to others – whether it's a school or home. For some, it's important to go to school, and for others, it's more important to live in a home.

Past Lifestyle. Each of the group members shared photos depicting previous lifestyle choices, some of which they recognized as having played a role in why they got locked up. Each of these young men expressed a changed lifestyle or a desire to change and be successful while on the outs.

It is notable that while the group members are making efforts to sustain these changes, their daily life circumstances and community surroundings have not necessarily changed with them. It is conceivable that this reality might contribute to an increased vulnerability to revert to old behaviors.

This left us wondering a few things. What could have been done to prevent their engagement in illegal activities and their time being incarcerated? And, what services are provided to strengthen their transition back to their communities and increase their likelihood of successful reentry?

Figure 11. Old Lifestyle. Basically what a joker does is make other's lives miserable – he does bad things like lie, steal, drugs. This is a joker I drew when I was in jail and it is my old lifestyle.

Figure 12. My Past.[3] I was a troublemaker, I liked guns a lot. This is just my past – used to get high every day. Now, I'm different – it's just my background.

---

[3] Please note that because of safety concerns, the image titled My Past was not shared at the gallery. Instead, a written description was included with the accompanying title and caption.

Figure 13. The Field. In this field is where I used to hang out when I was little, when I tried to get away from the cops and trouble. It's where I first tried coke.

Figure 14. Past. For most people, their past is left behind them, but it's different for some. For me, this helps remind me what happened back then, when it was hard for a child with bruises and welts.

Nature. Each of the group members took multiple pictures depicting their attraction to nature (e.g., animals, plants, scenery). Some of these photos are shown here. Their photos prompted discussion about the minimal access they had to such things while incarcerated and the ways that these are currently a positive aspect of their lives.

Figure 15. Life's Changes. Life comes in many forms and colors. Life shows age, hardships, irregularities. Life is hard at times, especially for those who get into trouble with the law and trying to change their ways, such as plants change color and size.

Figure 16. Firulice. This picture is just my dog. I got this picture because I love dogs. They are strengths because they're a friend and always help you stay out of trouble. I had a dog at [name of jail setting] and I was one of the few that was able to have a dog in there. It kept me company there once a week, it was fun teaching the dog tricks and doing the show I did.

Figure 17. Untitled.

Figure 18. Untitled.

Figure 19. Echo. This is my girlfriend's cat. I took this picture because when I see him I see nothing but beauty. That's my little baby.

Art and Music. The group members consistently expressed a love of both music and other art forms. These were common interests shared among these young men despite other differences.

Music was a weekly topic of discussion and fostered relationships. Each of the group members identified music as an important component of his life.

Art appeared to be a strength for each of the young men. They used various art mediums to express who they are, what is important to them, and also as an emotional outlet.

Figure 20. Strings and Harmony. I took this picture because of my love for music and my appreciation for those who play it.

Figure 21. Wu-Tang. This is my room. I love Wu-Tang. I drew Method Man in jail. I got a lot of memories on the wall, all my friends sign it. It's my "Wall of Fame."

Figure 22. Untitled.

Figure 23. Untitled.

Figure 24. Me. This picture represents me. I drew this picture in jail – cards because I always played cards, a car because I like cars, a skull with Locs because I always got my Locs, and the rest is just stuff I liked and was able to draw.

Our Support System. These pictures depict things that the participants identify as personally supporting them while on the outs. The young men recognized friends as being both a positive and a negative. Returning to their homes, they are often met with their friends that they were spending time with before going away, a potential lack of positive peers or peers at all.

The teachers they talked about as supporting them were described as personable, people they felt comfortable talking to and being around, people who were able to focus on the big picture and not dwell on the small, rigid details or rules, and those that kept classroom learning engaging and entertaining. They also said they liked those that gave them gifts, as they perceived their gift-giving as a sign that the person cared for them.

They recognized parole as causing them to think about their choices.

Figure 25. The 3rd Floor. I took this picture out of my favorite teacher's class. She's real cool – she's been there for me through my struggles and I go to her for advice.

Figure 26. My Little Brother. It's just a picture of him – I love him, do anything for him. I spend a lot of time with him, play a father figure, especially now since dad's gone. He didn't used to like me because I used to play rough when I first got out, but now it's just fun & he gives me kisses.

Figure 27. My Buddy. I took this picture because I love him, he's part of the family. My mom and dad love him, I take him everywhere. He's my baby. His name is Juagiddy because my coach from my placement was real cool to me, and that was his name.

Figure 28. Love. This is me and my girlfriend. We took this on the way to my house. I really like this picture because there is someone there for me who loves and cares for me and has my back no matter what. She's been my friend since fifth grade, and now she's my girlfriend.

Developing Our Creative Talents. There were several photographs throughout the gallery that did not have accompanying captions. These photos were taken by the group members because they found the images to be visually attractive. They also show their progressively developing photography skills and their experimentation with photography techniques.

Figure 29. Untitled.

Figure 30. Untitled.

Figure 31. Untitled.

Figure 32. Untitled.

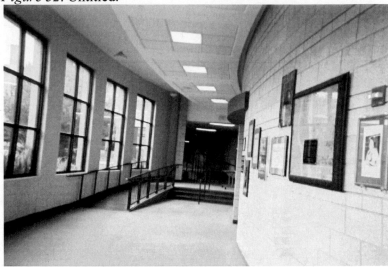

Figure 33. Untitled.

Figure 34. Untitled

Figure 35. Untitled

Figure 36. Untitled

Figure 37. Untitled

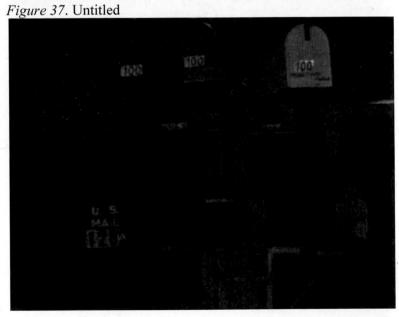

Figure 38. Untitled.

Figure 39. Untitled.

Figure 40. Untitled.

Figure 41. Untitled.

Figure 42. Untitled.

Retrospective Considerations of Photo Groupings

Through the processes of peer and expert review, as well as continued exploration of the data and personal reflection, there are a few points that I feel are notable with regard to the initial photo groupings. Please refer to the previous sections to view the images discussed here. In particular, I think it is notable that the image entitled Past (Figure 14) represents this young man's experience as a victim of abuse; this is a factor that he identified as having played a role in his subsequent illegal behavior. The photo grouping as a whole, *Past Lifestyle* (Figures 11-14), was constructed to highlight the risk factors that each of the group members photographed and therefore recognized to have contributed to their incarceration. While this experience coincides with this theme, the group descriptor and the title do not accurately portray his encounter because they suggest that the images represent lifestyle choices when, in fact, being the victim of repeated abuse was by no means his choice.

Secondly, it seems that more is being represented in the group entitled *Nature* (Figures 15-19) than the title suggests. The photographs were initially categorized because they depicted things in our natural environment that the group members were attracted to, but also had limited access to while incarcerated. In some ways, it was trying to point out their innate attraction to these things that are also lost along with their freedom in a secure setting; however, the group seems to represent more than that. Young people often view their world by identifying things of importance to them. Consequently, it seems that this section represents not only aspects of nature or loss, but things of particular value to the group members as well as additional supports in their lives.

Additionally, one photo grouping portrayed what the participants perceived to be supportive to their success. It is notable that although the group decided to title this section *Our Support System* (Figures 25-28), four of the five images were taken by one participant. In actuality, this group may also then suggests the minimal support felt by the other two group members.

Lastly, several people, including myself, have questioned the inclusion of the two images entitled Old Firefighters (Figure 9) and The School Speed Limit (Figure 10), suggesting that they do not seem to fit appropriately in the group *Strengths and Weaknesses of Our Community* (Figures 6-10) or any other section. The images have been included in an effort to respect the choice of the group member who photographed them and created their captions; however, it is remarkable that the images and their descriptors do feel out of place. I think that this accurately reflects the photographer who had difficulty expressing his ideas clearly and was often, himself, isolated or out of place. While the meaning that accompanies the images may not be clear or might even create some confusion, I think that this emulates the manner in which this young man is sometimes viewed or received by others. Furthermore, the inclusion of the images allows the reader to see how this participant views and conceptualizes his surroundings and the insight that follows these reflections is meaningful and relevant for better understanding this young man and his troubled life.

PART II: PARTICIPANT STORIES

I had initially planned to seek emergent themes from the various pieces of data collected (i.e., photos and captions, weekly notes, transcribed group sessions). However, as I conducted this process it became increasingly evident that strong group themes were not clearly present. Each participant approached the project in his own unique manner and shared elements of his personal life. Although similarities were noted, these were not always shared by all group members. Furthermore, I wanted to be careful not to overemphasize commonalities as themes. Through several consultation sessions with two qualitative researchers familiar with Photovoice, we decided that, in addition to the content shown at the gallery, it would be most appropriate to share the participants' individual stories. Although in-depth social histories were not formally conducted, a great deal of this information emerged throughout the research process. A similar finding was noted by Dixon and Hadjialexiou, (2005) who conducted a six-week Photovoice pilot study with young people experiencing homelessness in Australia.

The previous section provided a snapshot into the lives of these young men and highlighted who they were, how they spent their time, and what they had started to recognize as the strengths and weaknesses surrounding them. However, having spent several weeks with them, I also learned more about each of them than can be gleaned exclusively from their photographs and captions. Therefore, I present partial stories representing those things that each participant chose to share as a group member in this Photovoice research project. The decision to include this piece in the findings came as a result of continued consultation during the data analysis stage of the project. Because it was not anticipated at the outset, and contact with the participants was not maintained beyond the project completion, they have not read these stories. However, given Kristen's integral role throughout weekly meetings and her knowledge of the participants, she reviewed the stories for accuracy and provided additional feedback and insights. This information is intended to supplement the findings reported in the previous section, helping the reader to take a deeper look at the life experiences of these young men.

Marcus

"It was always hard for me to get a job after getting in trouble. Not many people want to hire someone who's been in trouble with the law." We listened as Marcus described one of his most creative photos. It was one of the only photos he shared that focused on employment, despite the fact that Marcus talked about work weekly. He had earned his GED while incarcerated and returned home in search of a job. This was the first time in his life that Marcus was seeking employment. One can imagine the challenges associated with this new life task. To make matters worse, Marcus believed that some employers held negative perceptions of him because he was on parole.

Lack of a job... How you go in for an interview, I have to tell them that I am on parole but I will be off soon. And then they go, well you can come back then...and then it also sets restrictions on whether you can apply then or not.

Marcus wrestled weekly with his ideas about work. His beliefs fluctuated in response to his experiences. One week Marcus highlighted the importance of knowing people in order to obtain work, a new perspective that he formed after a friend of the family gave him a job. This was one of the several positions that he found and obtained during our eight weeks together, experiences that contributed to his shifting perceptions of employment. He changed jobs quite often and was met with many difficulties in this area. Despite several set-backs, Marcus continued searching for work. Having been in secure facilities on and off for four years, it is conceivable that Marcus lacked opportunities to develop the skills needed to be successful in an employment context. This, combined with his inexperience and further compounded by the negative attributes associated with his time in confinement, reduced his ability to maintain the positions he was offered. At times he was unsure what was happening at work. Marcus' difficulties with work seemed to be in some ways related to his misunderstandings about the processes (e.g., applying, hiring, etc.) and misperceptions in his interpersonal interactions. This was obvious in his explanations that themselves were unclear.

For example, in one instance, Marcus shared that he had been hired but later realized that someone else had been given the position and he would be considered if it became available in the future. Another time Marcus was unclear whether or not he was still employed. He described his interaction with the manager, explaining that he thought that he may have been fired from the position for not working quickly enough when another employee was not there. Marcus' social skills and interpersonal mannerisms, combined with his lack of prior knowledge or experience, likely impeded his success. Unfortunately, the last time I saw him Marcus was no longer working at his most recent job, rendering him once again unemployed.

Money was a concern for Marcus, one he appropriately correlated with the importance of having a job. At the time of the project he lived with his mother and step-father but had hopes of moving out. He recognized the need to earn money in order to eventually have a place of his own. One might expect that a young man having spent several years under strict supervision would be reliant on others; however, Marcus was fairly independent. In addition to being motivated to have a job and get his own apartment, he relied on his bike for transportation. His bike was very important to him; yet interestingly, he never shared a photograph of it. Marcus seemed to be accustomed to being alone. In some ways, it presented as independence; however, taking a closer look, it appeared that he had no other alternative. He seemed to be missing the important elements of friendship, feeling connected to others, or being a part of something. There seemed to be something lacking in his life. Although he briefly mentioned a friend or two, Marcus never really described any friendships, again suggesting that limited social skills may have influenced his experiences in the community.

Many young people learn about and form lasting friendships during their teenage years. Marcus had spent the majority of his adolescence in state-run facilities. This reality left Marcus returning home to few, if any, friends. Imagine the challenges one might face returning home as an adult with limited opportunities during his adolescence to form peer relationships in the manner we would generally expect (e.g., at school, at work, in the neighborhood). In addition to having missed out on many of these types of opportunities, Marcus' social awkwardness was another barrier. Observing him in group, Marcus commonly exhibited behaviors that caused others discomfort. He arrived hours early, his comments were oftentimes difficult to follow, and at times he acted in ways that were much younger than his age.

He participated actively in group and even began to talk with the other members; however, he did not form a relationship with either of the other two group members. He also lacked common experiences that might contribute to conversations that could forge connections with others outside of group. It was easy to see how he might be rejected when he disclosed that he'd been incarcerated, perhaps even more so if he shared the length of time or reason for incarceration. If he did not reveal the details of this experience, what would he talk about? Even his experience with parole, a legal status intended to provide continued supervision upon return to the community, left Marcus guessing. He shared that this was his second parole officer and despite his best attempts to maintain contact with her, they had lost touch. It seemed like Marcus was moving through his life on his own with little or no support and guidance. For example, Marcus' mother explained that it was important he spend more time with his biological father; however, that same day, his father dropped him off at the art gallery without coming inside. There was no one in attendance to show their support for Marcus. Even his parole officer was absent.

This may have also been true for Marcus as a child. When his parents divorced, Marcus lived with his father and stepmother. He identified being away from his biological mother as one of the contributing factors in his illegal behavior. More so, he acknowledged his own experiences of victimization as playing a key role. Marcus shared his experience with the group, a story that was generated from an image that he took representing a piece of his childhood home.

> In '97 I moved back into this house 'cause my mom and my dad got a divorce when I was two or three and then I moved to [State] and lived with my grandmother and my mom until I was seven. When I was five I met [Step-mother] and not too long after that, a couple months...I started getting physically abused by her, and it actually ended when I was almost 13...Whenever I was 10 I moved back into my dad's house because he said to the judge my mom was neglecting me and didn't want to

take care of me, which was not true, 'cause she was stuck to a loser. And to this day my dad still doesn't believe that [Step-mother] physically abused me. I don't know why. I have a restraining order against her... I was physically and emotionally abused by her and her daughter [name]...I was sexually abused by her.

Research has provided significant support for the cycle of violence theory, which proposes that childhood maltreatment increases the risk for illegal behavior, especially violent offenses (Fagan, 2005). Marcus' recognized this reality in his own life.

Marcus returned home with hopes and dreams of a future. He considered numerous avenues for vocational training, employment, and higher education, some of which he actively pursued. Unfortunately, the risk factors (i.e., minimal experiences, inadequate social skills, history of mistreatment, limited support system, and legal history) in Marcus' life frequently created barriers to his success. As a participant, he consistently presented himself as responsible, persistent, and determined, characteristics that might support him in his future endeavors. My interactions with Marcus have inspired many questions. Most of all I wonder, what will become of this young man and what we can do to facilitate his success? Whose responsibility is it to help young people like Marcus when they return? If he does not have positive, supportive role models in his life, who will he turn to for guidance? And have we equipped him for a fresh start and positive outcomes, or have we simply added to the obstacles in his life?

Raul

Raul casually strolled into the facility meeting room, usually early, rarely late, and sometimes without his camera. He was always well-groomed and dressed in a certain style that aligned with stereotypical gang appearance – namely, shaved head, and oversized clothes – generally a dark blue Polo style shirt worn un-tucked and buttoned to the top, grey Dickies, and sneakers. He was a young man who, upon reentry into his community, was in many ways struggling to adapt his new-found identity with the environment he had left before his incarceration. Being locked up was a turning point in Raul's life; he seemed to recognize several ways that the experience had helped him, despite having its drawbacks. During his time away he achieved sobriety from methamphetamine, an addiction that he associated with his choices to engage in illegal behaviors and believed had taken control over his life. He shared,

> 'Cause that is how I got my last charge, 'cause I was smoking meth a lot and I decided to steal and that is how I got charged...Yeah, the last year was fucked up. It messes with your head a lot man.

In addition to sobriety, Raul also learned to draw for the first time, a skill that can be seen in some of his artwork that he photographed and an interest that has the potential to serve as a catalyst for a successful future. His image entitled "Past Lifestyle" is not only an example of his artistic talents, but exemplifies the way in which drawing and self-reflection are reciprocal for Raul.

Raul shared that he was trying not to "bang" as much as he used to but some aspects of the gang, such as peer associations and style of dress, could still be recognized in his choices. Despite his expressed decision to reduce his gang behaviors, Raul regularly placed himself in situations that may be considered high-risk (drinking and spending time with peers using illegal drugs) and being associated with and actively involved in physical altercations with gang associates. Raul seemed to look to his peers for guidance, although he did not recognize this behavior in himself. In group, Raul frequently checked in with Eduardo before answering questions posed to the entire group or, at times, simply agreed with Eduardo's responses rather than providing his own. He also shared that he disagreed with concerns expressed by his mother about his tendency to follow his friends.

As much as Raul stated a desire to make a "better life" for himself, it seemed as if he hadn't yet figured out what that meant, nor did he know how to accomplish the goal. In some ways, it was as if this was something he had been told by others, possibly staff he encountered during incarceration or his parole officer upon release, and was now beginning to integrate into his own ideals. Regardless, his choices did not always align with or support his expressed hopes. When asked about his drug use Raul responded,

> Well like for meth I don't want to do that shit again but like for weed like when I get off parole I don't know if I am going to get high or if I'm not 'cause I don't think weed is like a bad thing so yeah…I will probably start thinking about it when I am off parole.

Some would agree that using any illegal substance would place him at greater risk of relapse and using methamphetamines. It seemed that he was choosing not to smoke marijuana in order to meet the requirements set by his parole status. Conversely, Raul's intention to abstain from using methamphetamine appeared to be long-term and based on his recognition of the unfavorable ways his use had impaired his judgment and mental health, and interfered with his life. He may not have had the skills necessary to navigate risky situations like being around peers using illegal substances or to recognize the benefits of avoiding such situations altogether. His participation in the weekly group did offer a productive, positive alternative way to spend his time.

Raul spent a large portion of his time at home where he was responsible for the care of his younger brother, and sometimes his nephew, while other family members were at work. Similar to his experience with incarceration, this responsibility carried with it both positives, such as developing a strong, loving relationship with his younger brother, and negatives like feelings of boredom and being trapped. When his father moved out of state for work, the circumstances left Raul to take on a fatherly role. He began to contemplate dropping out of school in order to work, an option that he viewed as a solution to his concerns about money. The last time I met with him, Raul was still attending a local alternative high school and after having received many compliments and positive feedback about his photographed drawings by gallery attendees, he was considering attending college to study art.

While Raul expressed a great love and protection of his younger sibling, at the same time he seemed to feel unimportant in the eyes of his family and missed spending time with them. One evening everyone was asked to bring three personal items to share with the group. Raul forgot to bring his and instead was asked to share what he would have brought.

> I don't know. My imaginary fishing pole, I like to fish a lot. We used to [go around here] but since I got out it was already starting to get cold or sometimes it was cold. I don't know. My dad, we don't really go anymore.

This and other comments that he made about his family having "better things to do" than attend the gallery alluded that he was in some ways unhappy with his home life.

Unfortunately for Raul, school was no better. He attended an alternative high school where his sister was also a student. He rarely had good things to say about school. He found it rather frustrating that he had to wake up early to attend school where he was simply bored. He shared that the topics were generally not of interest to him and that some of the older teachers only relied on the chalk/white board for instructing. He did mention liking some of the classes that "helped him out" but it wasn't clear what exactly differentiated one from the other. Overall, it seemed that he did not have a bond with school or any of the teachers like he did with staff he had met while incarcerated. Raul asked to invite four staff members from the facility where he had stayed; in contrast, he did not express an interest in asking any of his teachers. He did not seem to have good relationships with his teachers, nor was the subject matter of interest or relevance to him. Finding ways to facilitate his engagement in the curriculum and school environment would likely support his transition; however, based on what he shared, this did not appear to be the reality of the circumstances.

Raul held strong negative feelings about the existence of racism within the legal system and the town where he lived. When speaking about his photo titled Easlos (Figure 4), the slang term he used for the park where he spent time with friends, Raul highlighted the observation that "most of the time there's always cops around there." For him, this heightened level of police presence in areas where Latinos gathered was part of the racism within his community. Raul shared that when he and his family moved into this section of the town, his was the only Latino family among a neighborhood of Whites. He explained that his White neighbors had since moved out of his neighborhood as if they were better than the Latinos. This experience angered Raul, as did his perceptions of racial mistreatment in the legal system. Raul perceived that judges were more likely to find Blacks and Latinos guilty; he described police as racist and crooked. He also felt that they targeted certain groups. "I think they are, they're more like out to get us. The gang unit...Try and bust us for no reason. Yeah, 'specially the Mexicans and the Blacks." He further described police as holding a level of power that allowed them a certain freedom in their interactions with people and protected them from consequences for behaving inappropriately or for mistreating people.

Raul was quite a talented artist. He returned home with this newly developed skill and hobby. He had been considering vocational training in mechanics; after the exhibit, he expressed an interest in attending college for art. Like the other group members, Raul faced several risk factors (i.e., low self-efficacy, fear of failure, lack of school engagement, gang involvement, history of addiction and incarceration), placing him at-risk for unfavorable outcomes (e.g., reincarceration, drug relapse). While he seemed to have left confinement wanting to make changes in his life, Raul returned home to many of the same situations he had been in prior to being locked up. He was trying to maintain friendships and his loyalty to his gang while at the same time decrease his active involvement and refrain from drug use. It seems like these would be much easier to do when he could use the excuse of being on parole in the face of peer pressure. I'm not so sure this will be an easy feat for him once off parole. What skills will he use to combat peer pressure? How do we help young people like Raul find and develop relationships with positive role models and supportive peers? What community services are available for him to continue building his skill set and engage in productive activities without experiencing reincarceration?

Eduardo

"I'm cool with everyone," Eduardo bragged, referring to his multiple friendships and his ability to have relationships with active and opposing gang members without being involved himself. I feel like I learned the least about Eduardo, although I am not sure why. He regularly engaged in group discussion and openly answered questions. He was honest about the role of marijuana in his life and his past "violent side" as he called it. Yet, for some reason, it seemed that overall his disclosure remained at the surface level. He frequently photographed and easily discussed his interests and likes. Toward the end of the project, he started to photograph images reflective of his incarceration experience.

During our work together, Kristin and I agreed that when describing his involvement with risky or illegal behaviors, Eduardo had a tendency to minimize the severity of the circumstances and/or his responsibility in the situation. For example, when describing events that resulted in probation, Eduardo called attention to the fact that these were unintentional or playful in nature.

> I pulled a knife out at a girl at the club, on accident, but she got all scared and called the cops on me. I got probation for that. Then I pulled a knife on my friend and he called the cops on me...He was my friend, but

then he wasn't really my friend. I was just messing
around with him.

Despite playing down his actions, Eduardo did recognize the
role of violence and drugs in his life and, in particular, made note
of his personal challenges with violent behavior.

This is my negative side – weed, violence. I got in
trouble for a gun. That is my friend's gun right there; I
took a picture of it. There's weed, a pipe. I used to get
high every day before I got locked up. I just loved it.
Now I don't like being around it. I don't get high. That's
my violent side. I used to have knives and swords and
guns and I don't care about that anymore. My friend has
a gun and I just wanted to take a picture of it.

I think that Eduardo truly wanted these aspects of his life to
remain a part of his past; unfortunately, he regularly surrounded
himself with peers who were not making the same choice,
thereby placing himself in risky situations for relapse. This quote
serves as a perfect example. Eduardo is sharing how he no longer
likes to be near marijuana, while at the same time showing his
friend's drugs and paraphernalia. This is similarly true of his
relationship with his girlfriend. Eduardo identified his girlfriend
as a strong support in his life, but also shared that she repeatedly
peer pressured him to smoke marijuana with her and always
carried marijuana and paraphernalia. Upon return to his
community, Eduardo seemed to have a newfound perspective on
his behaviors, yet was regularly confronted with peers and
situations that could easily challenge these changes. It is easy to
see how the influence of those around him might begin to break
down his new ideals over time.

On the contrary, it is also possible that his motivation and
love of school was supporting his movement towards a more
positive lifestyle. While incarcerated Eduardo earned many of
the credits he needed to graduate high school. When describing
what he liked about one particular facility he proudly shared,

"Healthy, study, I got all my credits done…Yup, I kept all my credits up. I'm going to graduate." Returning home excited about the prospects of graduation, Eduardo identified school as a strength in his life, photographing the physical structure and telling of his favorite teacher, "She's cool. She gives us candy and chips and stuff. She is cool." Eduardo was attending a local high school where he received special education services. He seemed to generally like school for both the learning and social aspects, but also faced academic challenges. When asked about these difficulties, he described the following experience with his class work and attempts to access help from his teachers. "Yeah, it's too hard…it's way too hard. They won't help you. I asked for help but they never respond. Can you help me with this? They just say do this, do that. I don't get it." After failed attempts to access help, Eduardo managed the situation by skipping or avoiding class, resulting in a failing grade.

Eduardo expressed consideration for attending college and also for becoming a police officer after graduation. He explained that he wanted to be the "cool cop" in the neighborhood. He, like Raul, perceived a racial divide in their community, which he described as "the nice part of town versus the ghetto." According to Eduardo, he lived in "the ghetto," which was frequented by police; as opposed to the other side of town, where he seldom spotted law enforcement. He held a strong contempt for police, describing them as racist, and believed that the legal system did not treat people of color with the same rights as Whites.

Friends, fashion, and music were the things that seemed to hold the most importance to Eduardo. He seemed to be quite popular among his peers and have strong family relationships. Many people attended the gallery in support of Eduardo. His photos frequently depicted pieces of his life that he liked. On the one hand, it seemed to offer him a way to minimize or avoid discussion of his previous experiences. Conversely, taking photos in this manner may have helped him to focus his attention on the strengths and positives in his life, perhaps helping him to explore alternatives to his previous life experiences and choices.

Eduardo strongly expressed a desire to make a different life for himself. While in jail, he seemed to develop values that contrasted with his past behaviors. Upon return, he was focusing on the many things in his life that he valued and enjoyed. While this may in some ways contribute to his continued minimization of past behaviors, it also suggests that he is seeking a new life and recognizing the value in his life outside of jail.

SUMMARY

As a whole, the stories and photographs that emerged through this process characterize daily life as experienced by these young men collectively and independently. I believe that the group members began to consider and better recognize the risk and protective factors in their lives while looking critically at the settings in which they interact. Their images speak to the hardships and successes they've encountered and represent the process of identity formation in the context of these experiences. The participants were actively thinking about their lives, reflecting on their past experiences and behaviors, and expressing hopes and desires to make positive life decisions.

CHAPTER 5
Insights into Juvenile Reentry

Juvenile crime is a problem with unfavorable outcomes for many. Most would agree that youth crime warrants further attention; however, all too frequently the focus on this problem takes the form of misinformation and distorted portrayals. Media depictions of young people who commit crimes are often one-sided, creating dramatic stories with the potential to elicit strong emotional reactions among audiences. Repeated exposures of this nature reinforce stereotypes about these young people, frequently painting them as lost causes, monsters, or unworthy criminals. Biased portrayals of this kind make it easy to blame these adolescents or their families and contribute to laws and policies that favor harsh punishments. There are, however, multiple aspects of crime that are additionally worthy of consideration. Many of these factors are beyond the control of the individual such as the effects of parental imprisonment, generational cycles of crime and gang affiliation, and the unfavorable life histories all too common among young people who become incarcerated. These experiences may include a host of adverse circumstances such as victimization, trauma exposure, addiction, family discord, mental health problems, and academic deficits. The hardships endured by those who commit crimes, as well as their families, are less well publicized or systematically researched. Because of this imbalance, the unique needs of this population are less known, allowing the underlying issues to go largely ignored. By neglecting the context of their lives, we inadvertently encourage the maintenance of stereotypes and the continued rejection of this group by the general public.

123

My purpose in completing this study was to give voice to young men reentering the community from a period of incarceration. They can teach us much about this phenomenon given their first-hand experience and knowledge about it. A gained understanding of the ways that they perceive their surroundings is one piece of the collective exploration needed to begin influencing social change in our communities. This study responds to calls by several researchers, including Bullis and Yovanoff (2002) who noted the following, "It is clear that much more research is needed to document the needs and challenges faced by incarcerated youth as they reenter society from the juvenile correctional system" (p. 76).

Photovoice is a participatory research strategy derived from Freirean theory, Feminism, and documentary photography. Freirean theory contends that any person, regardless of the degree of oppression, can look critically at his or her environment. Feminism purports that history is influenced by those with voice. The last element, documentary photography, is a technique that records phenomena using images taken by an outsider. Photovoice merges the strengths of these three by putting cameras in the hands of persons who have generally experienced marginalization in relation to mainstream society, such that they may share the way they view their surroundings. For the purposes of this Photovoice study, *Life on the Outs*, three adolescent males returning from incarceration took on this endeavor. These young men met for eight consecutive weeks to share images and experiences representative of their lives. The photos and discussions from these gatherings culminated in a photo gallery attended by a diverse group of friends, family, and community members, creating a unique opportunity for a dissimilar group of individuals to come together and interact during a shared experience and learn more about an issue that impacts all of us.

The foundational research goal that guided this study was to better understand the participants' perceptions and understandings of their surrounding community. More specifically, I wanted to know how they viewed themselves within different contexts, what factors they identified to be the strengths and weaknesses of their communities, and what, if any, community factors they believed to influence or maintain illegal activity. Increased awareness of this sort has the potential to counteract stereotypes and misconceptions, raise awareness of the struggles faced by these young men, and subsequently influence individual and systemic changes.

This Photovoice project created an opportunity for the group members to learn a new, healthy way of self-expression through photography, and employed a multisensory approach to research and participant engagement. The multisensory stimulation (e.g., tactile, kinesthetic, visual, etc.) inherent in this methodology, combined with the artistic elements, made it highly suitable for research with this population. Learning photography was appealing to the group members, and it motivated them to look actively at their lives and their surroundings upon reentry. Their photographs and discussion sessions provided an outlet and opportunity for self-reflection. It became one way for the participants to gain greater awareness of personal and community elements.

The images and stories they shared reflected their transition across three contextual situations: pre-incarceration, experiences in confinement, and the reentry process, bringing to light their perceptions and understandings of the risk and protective factors evident at each stage. Their images depicted what they saw as their past lifestyles, their most recent hopes and goals, developed in part as a result of being in state custody, and the challenges associated with merging the two upon return to their original settings.

It is easy for outsiders to recognize the negative outcomes associated with difficult situations such as incarceration; however, for some, adverse circumstances of this nature have the potential to simultaneously provide benefits that may go unnoticed by even a careful observer (Affleck & Tennen, 1996). I began this study with the understanding that we would be exploring crime from the perspective of young men. Yet I held the assumption that we would share the common goal of preventing or reducing incarceration and the view of incarceration as a negative outcome. In actuality, however, our perception of incarceration differed in that I viewed it as a negative outcome suggestive of the need for prevention efforts and services to help young people who might be vulnerable to the experience. From the participants' perspective, they identified negative components of the legal system and jail experience; however, when asked about their experience they articulated the view that incarceration might be appropriate for others like themselves because of the benefits witnessed in their experiences. This finding came as a surprise to me. The following are examples of the types of things they found helpful during incarceration: healthy living habits, educational gains, treatment for substance abuse and other physical or mental health problems, and learning new skills. Similar experiences were found by Todis, Bullis, Waintrup, Schultz, and D'Ambrosio (2001) who conducted a five-year qualitative study of resilience among formerly incarcerated adolescents. They too noted and highlighted "components of the correctional system that the respondents reported as positive for them: structure; classes and interventions; positive adult contact; and time to reflect and mature" (Todis et al., p. 130). These findings suggest that these adolescents appreciate the help they received and, moreover, indicate that they are in need of particular services and interventions. Furthermore, it may also imply a gap in access to interventions and programs within the community given that the group members viewed incarceration as an exclusive gateway to these services.

During this project the participants looked retrospectively at the lives they led prior to incarceration. It was greatly apparent from their images and captions, as well as group discussions, that their views about past behaviors and decisions had been challenged while away. Recognizing negative patterns of behavior that led to their present circumstances (e.g., incarceration) and acknowledging a need to modify those can initiate behavioral changes among youth in residential corrections (Abrams & Aguilar, 2005). In our study, the group identified several factors that contributed to their decisions to engage in illegal behaviors. They expressed these visually with images of places where drugs were used, items they surrounded themselves with such as weapons and drug paraphernalia, and symbolically with photos representing experienced victimization and negative peer associations. Participants commonly labeled this stage of their life in a way that differentiated it from their present selves (i.e., "joker lifestyle," "old lifestyle").

The participating members also shared images and stories about their experiences returning home from incarceration. They expressed a sense of happiness and optimism about their return, as well as hopes for their futures. Their images depicted a sense of reconnection with family members, friends or girlfriends, and other parts of their lives that were limited or prohibited while incarcerated (e.g., pets, stores, personal style choices). Images such as these recalled the losses incurred during incarceration, as well as the possible supports available to youth returning home. Each group member expressed a desire for a different and successful future. Not only were they considering how to pursue a different life path, they were also looking at their previous and current situations with a new outlook. Reintegrating into a cultural system with a new understanding and belief structure can present significant challenges to anyone. Maintaining those changes in thought and behavior patterns on the outs within a system that has not simultaneously changed can be a daunting task. Youthful offenders reportedly encounter situations similar to those experienced before treatment and have found it challenging to overcome negative behaviors (Mincey, Maldonado, Lacey & Thompson, 2008). The findings from the present study offer further insight into the types of circumstances encountered by the group members upon return.

From the perspective of the participants of our study, the transition back to their communities, schools, and families bears with it new responsibilities and demands such as having to help family members, the need for money and transportation, and the stipulations set forth by parole. One participant described the challenges he faced obtaining and keeping a job, which he believed to be related to his current and previous legal status. Similarly, other developmental responsibilities, such as the requirement to attend school, were identified. Noted challenges regarding school included having to independently wake up early and arrive to school on time, not seeing the relevance or value of material taught, lack of experiential classroom opportunities, mistreatment on the part of teachers, inability to access help regarding difficult class work or assignments, and the time commitment making it difficult to simultaneously have a job. I would additionally include the fact that each of the group members attending school earned at least one failing grade during the course of our time together; however, they felt that the adults in their lives (i.e., teachers, parole officer) focused their attention on the one problem area rather than acknowledging their achievements in other classes. Furthermore, knowing the young men and their situations, I understand that the grades earned were partially related to the above-mentioned struggles. Lastly, one group member regularly reported dealing with issues of boredom. While feelings of boredom may not on the surface suggest significant concerns, adolescent offenders, especially those with a history of drug or alcohol abuse, may have few experiences with prosocial leisure or recreational activities (Altschuler & Brash, 2004) or engagement in social situations without substances. Therefore, finding new positive ways to spend time may be difficult or even intimidating; being unsuccessful with these attempts might result in a return to old habits and behaviors. Considerations for how to conceptualize and address these findings are discussed next.

IMPLICATIONS

Young people who commit crimes resulting in confinement characteristically encounter a host of adverse life circumstances. In some instances, juvenile corrections is viewed as an intervention with the goal of restricting future criminal involvement. It is common, however, for offenders to repeatedly return to state's custody, suggesting the need for continued modifications in this service delivery system focused on remediating this outcome. However, little is known about reentry among formerly incarcerated juveniles (Mears & Travis, 2004). Youth perspectives about their transition back into the community is scarce in the research literature, resulting in a failure to inform practice as it relates to evidence-based interventions for this time period (Abrams, 2006). The findings from the present study add to this body of knowledge by providing visual entry into the daily lives of young men who recently returned home from a period of incarceration. Furthermore, the captions accompanying their images allow us to better comprehend their perspective on multiple issues that affect this process, thereby heightening our understanding of their needs.

Youth in juvenile corrections are disproportionately from underprivileged communities. Consequently, a discussion about the transition needs of these youth must include consideration of "the particular circumstances of youth development within disadvantaged communities from which such a disproportionate share of confined youth are drawn" (Sullivan, 2004, p. 57). There exist varying social skill sets, unwritten rules, and tools needed for success or survival within different subcultures (e.g., geographical settings, social classes). Additionally, juvenile offenders are more likely to return to communities where the likelihood of being incarcerated again is more probable. The reasons for this are innumerable. The Disproportionate Minority Contact initiative of the Juvenile Justice and Delinquency Prevention Act of 2002 called for the examination of potential contributors to the overrepresentation of youth of color at all stages of the juvenile justice processes, as well as the identification of strategies for reducing this disproportionality. Therefore, the heightened occurrence of contact with the legal system among youth of color is a problem recognized at the national level. From the perspective of the group members in this study, it seems that a racial divide, policing practices, and racial bias in court decision making were among the reasons contributing to this reality in their community. When taking a closer look, we find that there are additional factors, perhaps unrecognized by the group members who experience these as the norm, that contribute to higher crime rates in certain places.

It is important to recognize that the normalcy and values placed on certain behaviors in certain communities may not be endorsed or necessary among dominant cultures. For example, when asked why his friend chooses to carry a gun with him, Eduardo explained, "I think he carries it just to protect himself, but he got jumped one time and he just carries it now." This quote expresses the feelings of safety associated with possessing a gun, but also brings up the need to protect oneself from victimization, an experience that appeared to be commonplace among the participants in this study and many other youth involved with the juvenile justice processes. When looking at environmental influences through a different lens, we must be mindful of the purposes that certain behaviors serve in maintaining a person's livelihood, even when these may be starkly in contrast with our own beliefs or educational enlightenment about the issue. In other words, what I constitute as risks or vulnerabilities may be defined differently by the members within another subculture. One area deserving attention to this regard is the belief about personal determination playing a role in incarceration.

If these young men witness and experience violence among people who are similar to themselves in their own communities and feel the need to protect or keep themselves safe, this implies that they may not view the police as providing that service to them. In the case of our group, members described the exact opposite perception when they discussed their beliefs that law enforcement on the local Gang Unit purposely targeted youth of color, sometimes without reason. If young people feel that their legal involvement is reliant upon external forces, rather than personal choice, and that they must rely on their own means for safety, what incentive do they have to select alternative behaviors?

TRANSITION NEEDS

The findings from this study offered insights into the types of circumstances encountered by youth transitioning from juvenile corrections. Formerly incarcerated adolescents experience challenges upon reentry that they anticipate prior to release (Abrams, 2006; Fields, & Abrams, 2010). As previously mentioned, community dynamics are linked to the outcomes of youth. When we take a closer look at the structures and policies that dominate the context, we can form hypotheses about which components may contribute to, maintain, or prevent juvenile crime. Persons immersed in communities characterized by negative or adverse circumstances and value systems are likely to take on similar attributes. In the same regard, the opposite is true. Therefore, prevention of initial illegal behavior and recidivism must incorporate systemic variables.

Community Assessment

Every community possesses its own unique composition. When we take into account the continuum of values, religious beliefs, ethnic representation, socioeconomic status, educational programming, etc., it becomes clear that to suggest a broad-based strategy for reintegration seems inappropriate. If we are to enhance success among youth exiting confinement, it is essential that grassroots efforts be taken to evaluate the unique skills needed to function within the environment to which they are returning and to determine what resources are available or perhaps inaccessible in those places. In order to accurately determine these realities, a diverse group of individuals representing key stakeholders must work collaboratively. "In the field of children's mental health and juvenile justice, it is widely believed that that wraparound approach is superior to traditional, more fragmented, methods of service delivery" (Wilson, 2008). By increasing interagency collaboration, a more holistic understanding of the strengths and needs of youth offenders and their families can guide service delivery.

Schools. Previous research examining the predictors of youth incarceration has identified a number of school-related variables (Baltodano et al., 2005; Wang et al., 2005). At the same time, positive engagement in educational settings has been identified as a correlate with post-exit success (Bullis & Yovanoff, 2002). Therefore, the educational context, one which is perhaps the most consistent in the lives of children and adolescents, has great opportunity to play a key role in preventing the initiation and reengagement in crime among youth. Unfortunately, "schools typically do not embrace teaching young people with histories of offending" (Mears & Travis, 2004, p. 12). Instead, their return is more likely to be met with resistance and policies such as zero-tolerance may impede their return completely (Matvya, Lever, & Boyle, 2006).

The field of school psychology has recently called for a social justice approach to service delivery. Such an approach corresponds with a beginning shift towards a public health perspective, a more comprehensive model that presents opportunity to consider the ecological contexts encountered by youth and a greater focus on prevention (Rogers & O'Bryon, 2008). The overrepresentation of disempowered groups in youth jails implies that this is indeed a social justice issue. School psychologists as change agents in academic settings are in a critical position to influence the role schools play in the cycle of incarceration and reentry. Goldkind (2011) similarly called for the involvement of school social workers in this process given professional training in a wide range of areas that make them somewhat suited to support reengagement of committed youth within schools, among their families, and within the community. The following section addresses considerations for how school psychologists, school social workers, or other designated professionals serving educational settings might help public school systems and formerly incarcerated students alike during the process of school reentry.

Returning youth with educationally relevant disabilities and mental illness may present with internalizing and/or externalizing behaviors that can be easily misinterpreted by teachers or school personnel as being either defiant or oppositional (Wood, Wood, & Mullins, 2008). Therefore, policies related to behavior management may not coincide with best practices and unknowingly perpetuate problems rather than mitigate them. Key mental health professionals can begin to shed light on some of the unique challenges faced by these students. For example, youth involved with the legal system typically have a history of maladaptive coping mechanisms, low frustration tolerance in response to academic demands beyond their skill level, and may be managing medications with known side effects such as sleepiness (Wood et al.). Evaluating the unique educational needs of returnees, facilitating interagency collaboration and partnerships with families, and providing professional development trainings and consultation to teachers are among the ways schools can support juvenile reentry.

Multidisciplinary teams familiar with the distinctive learning, behavioral, and mental health needs of returnees can also help in the development of appropriate educational programming designed to meet the unique needs of returnees. One important component in this feat is facilitating consistent and pertinent communication between correctional facilities and community-based educational settings. Partnerships of this nature are critical to the reentry process (Roy-Steven, 2004). The characteristic of disorganization within the juvenile justice system (Champion, 2007) suggests the difficulties of further bridging communications with key outside services such as schools; however, records from both systems can inform appropriate decision making. Recommendations for educational programming include comprehensive, integrated services. More specifically, consideration should be given to the inclusion of a health care plan, counseling or mental health services, family involvement and teacher education, as well as psychoeducation in areas of identified need (e.g., substance abuse, smoking cessation, stress management, effective communication; Wood et al., 2008).

Additionally, upon entrance into juvenile corrections, it is common for youth to have encountered a myriad of unfavorable experiences within the educational setting (i.e., failing grades, suspensions, etc.). As a result, they may equally be resistant to school or perceive it as an aversive setting upon return. Therefore, it is important that individual schools create opportunities and experiences that challenge such a view and instead promote the success of returnees. One way to go about this might be to form a support group for students who have experienced incarceration or to develop a mentor program between teachers and returning students. Participating teachers could be educated about the unique educational needs of this population and be informed of strategies for increasing their successful reengagement with school. This could also include facilitating engagement in prosocial activities and with positive peers. Many youth who offend are not acquainted with prosocial activities as ways to spend their free time and might otherwise revert back to old habits such as drug use or crime (Mears & Travis, 2004). Students who are reintegrating into the setting could be paired with these educators to better assist their transition back to school. They might teach them how to advocate for their own needs in that setting and help initiate their involvement in school activities such as clubs and sport teams.

Another way to support these young people is to begin building connections and working relationships with community service providers such as probation and parole officers. Although there is minimal research evaluating the effectiveness of these efforts, Matvya et al. (2006) described a number of model programs used throughout the US that promote successful reintegration. One such program in Pennsylvania uses school-based probation officers, in addition to those assigned by the court system, to look after the daily activities of adjudicated youth.

Issues that perpetuate crime and educational failure are not independent of systemic variables that extend beyond the school setting. A reciprocal relationship, for example, exists between the values and beliefs held by the dominant culture in an area and the practices they employ in their schools. Therefore, in order to influence and maintain social change at large, adaptations in beliefs and practices must extend into the community. Informed professionals can play a vital role in raising awareness of these salient issues and helping to bring together key stakeholders to collectively evaluate aspects of the community that maintain and prevent the continuum of youth crime.

Vocational assistance. Youth who reenter the community as emerging adults are faced with new responsibilities (Inderbitzin, 2009), one of which is financial independence. Most youth offenders aged 16 and older do not return to school or earn a high school diploma (Gemignani, 1994). Without adequate educational preparation, entry into the labor market is highly restricted. Adding to this challenge is the fact that these young adults may have few, if any, marketable skills, minimal work experience in legitimate settings, and carry with them the stigma and stereotypes associated with incarceration (Sullivan, 2004). Moreover, given the heightened rates of incarceration among young people from disadvantaged communities, the availability of employment prospects upon return is likely to be limited.

As in the case of school, engagement in employment has been identified as a correlate to success upon release (Bullis & Yovanoff, 2002). It is clear, however, that a number of barriers exist that may preclude a young person's ability to obtain and/or maintain work. Providing opportunities for employment is a common strategy used to discontinue illegal behaviors and incarceration among youth who offend (Office of Juvenile Justice and Delinquency Prevention [OJJDP], 2004). However, research evaluating the effectiveness of such programs has been mixed (OJJDP). Despite mixed reviews, vocational training continues to be recognized as a necessary step in preparing incarcerated youth to transition into the community (Matvya et al., 2006). Researchers have suggested the need for improved job training and vocational skills development (Inderbitzin, 2009) and recommended possible strategies such as involvement in One-Stop Centers that create a single point of entry for returnees entering the workforce (Altschuler & Brash, 2004). The OJJDP has also included vocational/job training in its Model Programs

Guide, a database of evidence-based programs regarding juvenile justice. There appears to be a general consensus that such programming is warranted, and that further scrutiny is needed to inform program developments and intervention services (OJJDP).

Family. Families play an integral role in the trajectory of youth development throughout the lifespan. Numerous studies have explored the characteristics of family systems that contribute to or mitigate antisocial behavior and juvenile delinquency (Thornberry et al., 2003; Thornberry, Smith, Rivera, Huizinga, & Stouthamer-Loeber, 1999; Walker-Barnes & Mason, 2004). On the other hand, the psychosocial impact of youth incarceration on family members has been vastly understudied. Actually, with the exception of one recent study by Church, MacNeil, Martin, and Nelson-Gardell (2009), "nothing has been examined about family dynamics during this critical time period, and therefore no interventions to facilitate successful negotiations among family members undergoing this experience have been developed" (p. 11). Church et al. conducted in-depth interviews with 11 primary caregivers whose children were detained, finding that many reported having strong, positive relationships with their youth prior to detention and were surprised and troubled to learn of their illegal behavior. Furthermore, they noted that family members were not excluded from the impacts of the youth's detention. For example, caregivers expressed frustration, sorting out misinformation about the legal standing of their child and feelings of confusion regarding their interactions with juvenile justice officials. Additionally, the circumstances resulted in daily life adjustments that families may have not been prepared for such as negotiating alternative child-care for younger siblings in the adolescent's absence.

The perception of parental involvement on the part of juvenile justice officials was explored in Ontario, Canada on the basis of the supposition that such beliefs are likely to influence or shape the processes of involving parents in youth legal proceedings (Peterson-Badali & Broeking, 2009). Semi-structured interviews revealed that legislation theoretically underscores parental involvement, but generally fails to incorporate parental participation in practice. Two themes noted officials' recognition of the need for parental involvement in advocating for the rights of children and the need for supervision of youth behavior and/or supporting behavior change. Parent involvement was seen as more or less important depending on the stage of justice proceedings (e.g., arrest, court, release points). Perceptions of this nature may very well influence the manner in which justice professionals reach out to parents and the types of efforts made in this regard, thereby influencing the role of caregivers in their child's legal processes as well as their own experience with the youth justice system. Continued research is needed to explore the experiences of families when a child becomes involved with the juvenile justice system.

Upon release, many young people return home to live with their families; therefore, including family members in treatment may be one way to strengthen and prepare the environment for a successful return. The OJJDP's (2004) Model Programs Guide listed family therapy, defined as "...family strengthening interventions [that] include family skills training, family education, family therapy, family services, and family preservation programs" (OJJDP) as effective prior to placement in a secure/residential placement or reentry. The Family Integrated Transitions (FIT) program, however, is recognized for use during the reentry phase. This program utilizes integrated individual and family services to support young people reentering the community with mental health problems and/or substance addiction. Furthermore, recent studies have demonstrated a reduction in recidivism rates through community-based wraparound services with former juvenile offenders who have emotional and behavioral disorders and their families (Pullmann et al., 2006). Interventions and services that include family may strengthen the overall outcomes for youth returning to the community as well as the family system as a whole. Clearly, there appear to be many promising avenues of reentry service provision and a strong need for continued research in this area seems quite appropriate.

LIFE ON THE OUTS: IDENTIFIED OUTCOMES

After completing a project of this intensity, it is important to reflect on what worked well and not so well. The following explores findings from the perspective of multiple individuals who were involved with this experience and how these may relate to previous projects as well as inform future Photovoice projects.

Participants of this study seemed to more easily photoraph issues and strengths of immediate relevance to them and had greater difficulty expanding to critically assess these aspects within their surroundings. In spite of specific discussion about their role as researchers, the purposes of Photovoice, and what creates a community, the group members frequently referred to our group as their "photography class," suggesting that perhaps the initial focus on developing photography skills sends the wrong message to group members (Dixon & Hadjialexiou, 2005).

Dixon and Hadjialexiou (2005) conducted a pilot study using Photovoice among youth experiencing homelessness. In their discussion, they acknowledged that the study participants exhibited some resistance transitioning from a focus on the technical aspects of photography to discussion surrounding opinions and attitudes. They hypothesized that this trouble was related to an initial emphasis placed on photography rather than explicitly communicating that group members would also be encouraged to talk about their perspective on issues of importance. Strack et al. (2004) addressed comparable findings when exploring the use of Photovoice with youth participants. They too noted an initial tendency toward taking images depicting people and things of direct personal significance as opposed to community aspects. In response, they encouraged the participants to use photography to describe themselves and their lives; they also challenged members who were developmentally advanced to incorporate social constructs amidst their images.

Researchers must consider the developmental appropriateness of Photovoice with youth and methods for adaptation that enable them to participate fully. Images of personal relevance, rather than the community at large, appear to be aligned with the developmental stage of adolescence and the process of identify formation that occurs during that period. This also seems to suggest something about young people's perceptions being possibly restricted, either as a symptom of their experiences of oppression or in relation to the minimal power that children and adolescents historically hold within contemporary America. Looking critically at oneself and immediate surroundings seem to lay the foundation for expansion to include greater social and political contexts. It seems that teaching critical thinking and exploration as it directly relates to their lives may be an initial stage toward empowerment among young people who have otherwise experienced oppression, lack of power, and hence may not initially equate their own beliefs and perceptions with social change.

In our group, the members at times struggled to believe that they might have the power to instigate change. During a group discussion about teachers, participants easily expressed their positive experiences and challenges with teachers and the characteristics that they liked and disliked in teachers. However, when asked for their suggestions or ideas about how to improve the problems, one participant responded by saying, "So like what's the point? You can't really change the teachers…it's their personality. It's hard when it's a person's personality. They have been like that for years." Another group member encouraged him by attempting to explain how he might depict this in an image and thereby instigate change. "It's kind of like that kid did when he was taking pictures of the ceiling [referring to a previous example from another Photovoice project]. If you see a teacher yelling, you take a picture of that person yelling." Clearly, he understood the general concept and was attempting to help another group member understand how highlighting or pointing out an issue can sometimes be enough to create even small change.

One of the intended outcomes of Photovoice is to facilitate social action or bring about increased awareness of the need for action. The vastness of results mirrors the diversity of Photovoice projects. In several studies, Photovoice has been used as a needs assessment among recipients of certain services. Information gathered under these circumstances is subsequently presented to a receptive, invested audience with the potential to respond immediately. The present study was conducted independent of an immediate service provider or direct link to policy makers or community members; therefore, assessing the outcomes by way of observed changes in policy or collective community action was more difficult. Conversely, it is important to note a number of concrete, smaller happenings that resulted from this work.

The photo gallery, and the project in general, resulted in an increased awareness among community members, the initiation of conversations surrounding the experiences of these young men, and insight gained by persons in attendance needed to initiate socially-relevant changes. A journal was used to collect written comments, many of which share the perceptions and reflections of gallery attendees. For example, one community member shared the following in his native language:

> *Yo pienso que la presentacion de los fotos fue una casa muy marabiyosa. Yo vine aver como eran los fotos pero lo que me impacto mucho son las istorias que estan atravez de los fotos. Cada foto tiene una historia muy importante y interesante que nadien podra imaginarselo. Tambien tienen unos sintimientos muy profundos. Fué una presentacion muy organizada ojala que la buelvan hacer porque fue muy interesante y apropiada. Han logrado muchos obstaculos y seguiran lograndolos.*

Additionally, one young man in attendance commented about how his friend's images spoke of his own experiences: "Eduardo's pics were off da wall and rep him and about what a lot of us are and what we go threw. Keep up da good work G!"

Positive attention or public recognition like that of the gallery is rare among youth returning from incarceration and others like them. It is possible that seeing Eduardo, a friend with whom he identifies, participate in this project can change this attendee's views about his own opportunities and self-expression. Another example of gained insight resulted from an opportunity for jail staff to see the young men in a different light. One invited staff member remarked,

> All of you guys did an amazing job with the pics. It's nice to see all of you doing this well, since all I remember of you is green scrubs! Keep your heads up & Keep workin. Talk to you kids later.

Because of confidentiality and policies, when youth leave the secure confinement setting their ties are usually broken with adults with whom they have developed relationships in juvenile corrections. Therefore, it is not common for workers to see them in any other capacity, a reality that may very well limit their perception and influence their interactions. Having a constructive opportunity to interact with youth on the outs who are doing well may provide a sense of hope or influence his practices at work.

After the gallery, one of the professors in attendance offered to communicate the details of the exhibit to the campus community electronically. Subsequently, I was contacted by a journalist for the local newspaper who had learned of the project on the campus website. We arranged for an interview to take place with the group facilitators and participating members, culminating in a newspaper article published on the front page of the local paper. I was also invited to speak to a graduate-level qualitative research class about the project. I made arrangements to meet with the journalist and class on the same evening amid the standing exhibit. One of the participants joined us, sharing his experiences and answering questions posed by the reporter and class members. Some of the graduate students in attendance wrote in a small notebook used to collect comments. The comments tended to address how viewing this gallery had greatly expanded their conceptualization of qualitative research and what it really means to provide an incentive for participants of research studies. For example one student wrote,

> The project was inspiring, both as a Doc student trying to put together my dissertation ideas, and to see that qualitative research really can deliver what it purports – a personal, in depth glance at the lives, feelings, & thoughts of people who are important in our field and have much to contribute to our understanding of the issue at hand.

Another student shared,

> Your reflection on how research has the potential to change the researcher and the participants' lives is most intriguing to me. The impact of being involved in research such as this seems to almost out-weigh the finding of the answer to research questions.

Furthermore, as a group, they noted a newfound consideration of photography as a data collection tool and identified the powerful nature of the participants' stories when expressed visually.

This increased awareness occurred through less formal avenues as well. At the initial gallery, two attendees, the superintendent of local area schools and another staff member of the local juvenile correctional facility, each expressed an intention to share their experiences at the gallery with others with whom they worked. The facility where our weekly meetings were held expressed ongoing support for our project and cultivating creativity and artistic skills among youth in the community. At the conclusion of the project they shared their intention to create an art studio at their facility to begin encouraging and facilitating engagement in art among attending youth. Finally, I received an unsolicited letter from the Region Program Manager for the Division of Youth Corrections (DYC) where this study took place. This letter serves as an example of

the scarcity of outreach and connection experienced by young
people involved with the legal process.

> On behalf of our [county] DYC office staff I would like
> to express my appreciation for the opportunity you and
> UNC have provided to the DYC parolees involved in
> your project. It is, sadly, uncommon for the community
> to reach out to our clients. Through your efforts these
> young men were able to engage in an activity that not
> only provided them a pro-social activity but also
> exposed them to the possibility of a lifetime interest they
> can pursue. One of the greatest challenges our parolees
> face is finding ways to spend time in ways other than the
> self-destructive and anti-social ways they have learned in
> the past. Further, the simple act of observation and
> reflection cannot help but broaden their horizons.
> Thanks again for you efforts and best of luck in your
> future endeavors.

LIMITATIONS

Research provides gained insights and fosters new questions
needing exploration. Inherent within this process is the presence
of limitations. The following section discusses limitations
identified in the present study. Participants of this project
generally took between 16 and 24 images per week. Once a
member had returned his images, he chose three to share with the
group for discussion. This number allowed for a manageable
group discussion; however, in retrospect, I recognize that a
larger number of images were not shared, representing a host of
data that may have added value and insight that remains
unknown in its absence. In order to address this limitation, future
Photovoice studies may seek to minimize the exclusion of
images and explore creative ways to include the breadth of
images taken in a manner that aligns with overall project goals.
For example, group discussion may still be limited to a smaller,
more manageable number of images, but include the addition of
individual meetings with each participant to explore the

remaining photographs. In order to maintain the principle of participant selection, group members should still choose which images to display during group or publicly. The images taken and not taken tell us about the participants. In a way, Photovoice participants are documenting their current living situations and perspectives through visual imagery.

There is great potential for the use of their photos to guide interviews; therefore, research investigating the use of images as a tool for interviewing is warranted. In Photovoice studies, this might be used to supplement information gathered through the traditional process. "Photographs of ourselves, our family albums, images of places we have been to – all of these build a picture of whom we are as people" (Fairey, 2010). In non-Photovoice research, photographs taken by participants or saved as keepsakes could be used either to guide life history interviewing or to elicit information regarding the historical context of a person's life.

Strack et al. (2004) recommended a small, manageable group size (i.e., youth to adult ratio of 5:1 or less) for conducting Photovoice with youth participants. This suggestion was based on the intense nature of Photovoice projects and the premise that groups of this size would allow for a setting more conducive to a successful and quality experience (Strack et al.). One thing to consider with a smaller number of participants is the make-up of the group members and how this may or may not influence the findings. In this study, two of the three members were of Latino descent, lived in the same neighborhood, and were members of the same peer network. Therefore, they shared certain experiences and commonalities that were distinctly different from the third member. These differences created a division in group findings that I believe contributed to some of the difficulties encountered in identifying themes. Therefore, small groups may want to consider having either a homogonous or heterogeneous group, but use caution with having only some members who share such close similarities or a single participant whose experiences are distinctly dissimilar than the majority.

Lastly, when thinking about the use of photographs as data, it is appropriate to consider the types of images that may not be taken and the potential barriers inherent in expressing oneself through photography. For example, participants may choose to photograph certain aspects of their lives in order to portray a certain image or mask a part of their life. On the other hand, we must consider whether the exclusion of certain images implies anything about aspects missing from an individual's life or rather things of less value to them. Lastly, the participants may have chosen not to take certain images for a number of reasons (e.g., beliefs about how their peers would react, safety concerns or possible incrimination, etc.). For example, photo ethics were discussed throughout this project. As part of this process, the group members were asked to use a Photo Consent form to obtain permission before photographing other persons. One member felt that this form was "stupid"; having to use it may have discouraged the group members from taking photos of people. Overall, it seems to be worthwhile to keep in mind that the images gathered are representative of the life circumstances that a participant chooses to share and, as with any research, does not necessarily represent the whole picture.

FUTURE RESEARCH

Photovoice methodology seems to have an inherent therapeutic component. Fairey (2010) conceptualized PhotoVoice as a therapeutic photography technique used globally with marginalized populations, and explained the beneficial consequences thusly:

> The potential when working with therapeutic photography lies not only in how we can use the camera to know ourselves better and to represent our impressions and experiences to each other, but also in the benefits it offers when people come together to learn new skills and offer each other support and appreciation.

Photography presents an effective catalyst for individual members to begin looking critically at their surroundings. This stage in and of itself carries with it the possibility for gained self-reflection and self-awareness, as well as serving as a vehicle to guide discussion around issues of concern or interest. Hanna, Hanna, and Keys (1999) recommended using "a variety of media" when conducting counseling with difficult or defiant adolescents because this approach enables self-expression without sole reliance on verbal skills. Sharing this experience in a group presents a number of additional therapeutic possibilities, including but not limited to a sense of normalization surrounding difficult life experiences, gained insights about positive coping mechanisms used by others to whom they can relate, and an opportunity to challenge cognitive distortions or mismatch between expressed desires and current behaviors.

Photovoice as a research methodology allows for a reduction in the power differential between the researcher and participating members, creating an experience for each to learn from the other. This concept can similarly be applied to a counseling relationship with people who have experienced oppression, in which both the client and counselor are viewed as co-learners (Hanna, Talley, & Guindon, 2000). "This involves the parties gaining knowledge from each other, each being equally enriched by the other's perceptions, knowledge, and experiences" (Hanna et al., p. 439). As such, the use of Photovoice or an adaptation of this process for the purposes of therapy deserves future study.

For use with young people returning to their communities from placement in juvenile corrections, I recommend including the following techniques. First, it is not uncommon for youth involved with the legal system to have a history of negative interactions with adults or others in a position of authority or power. Therefore, an initial focus should be placed on building a relationship founded on unconditional positive regard in which the client's strengths are emphasized and the person is accepted regardless of previous or present behaviors. This, in and of itself, has therapeutic implications for some youth. Secondly, "youth returning to their homes after their commitment to a juvenile

custody facility bring with them track records of failure..."
(Snyder, 2004, p. 54); therefore, helping these youth to recognize
their successes, skills, and potential should be a goal of therapy.
Cognitive-behavioral treatment (CBT) is a strategy
recommended for reentry by the OJJDP Model Programs
(OJJDP, 2004). When working with youth post-incarceration,
CBT can be employed to support changes in maladaptive
thought processes and behaviors. Additionally, incorporating a
focus on the development of internal locus of control and self-
efficacy seems appropriate for empowering youth, but also
helping them to actualize their potential and achieve success on
the outs. Furthermore, it may be beneficial to explore the use of
this technique within families, a subsystem that is additionally
affected by the episode of incarceration as well as the post-
incarceration transition. Such an approach may provide insights
for developing individualized transition programs to best meet
the unique needs of youth and their families, as well as helping
to increase their chances of successful reentry.

Future researchers may consider replicating a Photovoice
study among young women involved with the juvenile justice
processes. Reports made by Snyder and Sickmund (2006)
identified both similarities and differences between male and
female offenders. Given this fact, the day-to-day experiences and
perceptions of females that influence their involvement may also
vary, and this difference is worthy of exploration. Upon exit,
young women may similarly encounter the struggles of identity
formation; yet their coping mechanisms and beliefs about
community assets and problems may provide further insight and
knowledge about the reentry process among formerly
incarcerated adolescents. Currently, the research literature is
even scarcer with regard to female offenders than it is about their
male counterparts. Additional avenues for replication include
conducting Photovoice projects with youth participants who
receive services from existing community programs in order to
gain insights about their experiences utilizing such services and
inform ways to adapt components that may be less helpful and
build on well-suited aspects.

FINAL THOUGHTS

Before beginning this project, I had envisioned that this work might help participating members begin or continue down a new life path. At the conclusion, I believe that what we have done instead is more powerful – we have helped them and others begin to see their current path through a new lens.

Figure 43. Life on the Outs Photovoice Gallery.

"While there is perhaps a province in which the photograph can tell us nothing more than what we see with our own eyes, there is another in which it proves to us how little our eyes permit us to see."

~Dorothea Lange

References

Abrams, L. S. (2006). From corrections to community: Youth offenders' perceptions of the challenges of transition. *Journal of Offender Rehabilitation, 44*(2/3), 31-53.

Abrams, L. S., & Aguilar, J. P. (2005). Negative trends, possible selves, and behavior change: A qualitative study of juvenile offenders in residential treatment. *Qualitative Social Work, 4*(2), 175-196.

Affleck, G., & Tennen, H. (1996). Construing benefits from adversity: Adaptational significance and dispositional underpinnings. *Journal of Personality, 64*(4), 899-922.

Allen, J. P., Porter, M. R., & McFarland, F. C. (2006). Leaders and followers in adolescent close friendships: Susceptibility to peer influence as a predictor of risky behavior, friendship, instability, and depression. *Development and Psychopathology, 18*, 155-172.

Altschuler, D. M., & Brash, R. (2004). Adolescent and teenage offenders confronting the challenges and opportunities of reentry. *Youth Violence and Juvenile Justice, 2*(1), 72-87.

Archwamety, T., & Katsiyannis, A. (1998). Factors related to recidivism among delinquent females at a state correctional facility [Electronic version]. *Journal of Child and Family Studies, 7*(1), 59-67.

Arnstein, L. M., & Brown, R. T. (2005). Providing neuropsychological services to children exposed prenatally and perinatally to neurotoxins and deprivation. In R. C. D'Amato, E. Fletcher-Janzen, & C. R. Reynolds (Eds.), *Handbook of school neuropsychology* (pp. 574-595). Hoboken, NJ: John Wiley & Sons.

Bailey, C. A. (2007). *A guide to qualitative field research* (2nd ed.). Thousand Oaks, CA: Pine Forge Press.

Baltodano, H. M., Harris, P. J., & Rutherford, R. B. (2005). Academic achievement in juvenile corrections: Examining the impact of age, ethnicity and disability. *Education and Treatment of Children, 28*, 361-379.

Bandura, A. (1986). *Social foundations of thought and action: A social cognitive theory.* Englewood Cliffs, NJ: Prentice-Hall.

Bandura, A. (2006). Toward a psychology of human agency [Electronic version]. *Perspectives on Psychological Science, 1*(2), 164-180.

Beebe, M. C., & Mueller, F. (1993). Categorical offenses of juvenile delinquents and the relationship to achievement. *Journal of Correctional Education, 44*, 193-198.

Brier, N. (1989). The relationship between learning disability and delinquency: A review and reappraisal. *Journal of Learning Disabilities, 22*, 546-553.

Brody, G. H., Ge, X., Conger, R., Gibbons, F. X., Murry, V. M., Gerrard, M., et al. (2001). The influence of neighborhood disadvantage, collective socialization, and parenting on African American children's affiliation with deviant peers. *Child Development, 72*(4), 1231-1246.

Bronfenbrenner, U. (1979). *The ecology of human development: Experiments by nature and design.* Cambridge, MA: Harvard University Press.

Bullis, M., & Yovanoff, P. (2002). Those who do not return: Correlates of the work and school engagement of formerly incarcerated youth who remain in the community. *Journal of Emotional and Behavioral Disorders, 10*(2), 66-79.

Bullis, M., & Yovanoff, P. (2005). More alike than different? Comparison of formerly incarcerated youth with and without disabilities. *Journal of Child and Family Studies, 14*(1), 127-139.

Bullis, M., Yovanoff, P., & Havel, E. (2004). The importance of getting started right: Further examination of the facility-to-community transition of formerly incarcerated youth. *The Journal of Special Education, 38*, 80-94.

Bullis, M., Yovanoff, P., Mueller, G., & Havel, E. (2002). Life on the "outs" – Examination of the facility-to-community transition of incarcerated youth. *Exceptional Children, 69*(1), 7-22.

Burton, V. S., Cullen, F. T., & Evans, D. T. (1995). The impact of parental controls on delinquency. *Journal of Criminal Justice, 23*, 111-126.

Byrd, R. S., Weitzman, M., & Auinger, P. (1997). Increased behavior problems associated with delayed school entry and delayed school progress. *Pediatrics, 100*, 654-661.

Campbell, C., & Schwarz, D. F. (1996). Prevalence and impact of exposure to interpersonal violence among suburban and urban middle school students. *Pediatrics, 98*(3), 396-402.

Cauffman, E. (2008). Understanding the female offender. *The Future of Children, 18*(2), 119-142.

Champion, D. J. (2007). *The juvenile justice system: Delinquency, processing, and the law 5th Edition.* New Jersey: Pearson Prentice Hall.

Chung, H. L., & Steinberg, L. (2006). Relations between neighborhood factors, parenting behaviors, peer deviance, and delinquency among serious juvenile offenders. *Developmental Psychology, 42*, 319-331.

Church II, W. T., MacNeil, G., Martin, S. S., & Nelson-Gardell, D. (2009). What do you mean my child is in custody? A qualitative study of parental response to the detention of their child. *Journal of Family Social Work, 12*, 9-24.

Clark, H. G., Mathur, S. R., & Helding, B. (2011). Transition services for juvenile detainees with disabilities: Findings on recidivism. *Education and Treatment of Children, 34*(4), 511-529.

Cooley-Quille, M., Boyd, R. C., Frantz, E., & Walsh, J. (2001). Emotional and behavioral impact of exposure to community violence in inner-city adolescents. *Journal of Clinical Child Psychology, 30*, 199-206.

Creswell, J. W. (2007). *Qualitative inquiry and research design: Choosing among five traditions* (2nd ed.). Thousand Oaks, CA: Sage.

Creswell, J. W. (2009). *Research design: Qualitative, quantitative, and mixed methods approaches.* Thousand Oaks, CA: Sage.

Deptula, D. P., & Cohen, R. (2004). Aggressive, rejected, and delinquent children and adolescents: A comparison of their friendships. *Aggression and Violent Behavior, 9*, 75-104.

Diagnostic and statistical manual of mental disorders: Text revision (4th ed.). (2000). Arlington, VA: American Psychiatric Association.

Dishion, T. J., Spracklen, K. M., Andrews, D. W., & Patterson, G. R. (1996). Deviancy training in male adolescent friendships. *Behavior Therapy, 27*, 373-390.

Dixon, M., & Hadjialexiou, M. (2005). Photovoice: Promising practice in engaging youth who are homeless. *Youth Studies Australia, 24*(2), 52-56.

Drakeford, W. (2002). The impact of an intensive program to increase the literacy skills of youth confined to juvenile corrections. *Journal of Correctional Education, 53*(4), 139-144.

Duffy, K. G., & Wong, F. Y. (2003). *Community psychology* (3rd ed.). New Jersey: Pearson Education, Inc. (Original work published 1996).

DuRant, R. H., Cadenhead, C., Pendergrast, R. A., Slavens, G., & Linder, C. W. (1994). Factors associated with the use of violence among urban Black adolescents. *American Journal of Public Health, 84*, 612-617.

Eder, D., & Fingerson, L. (2002). Interviewing children and adolescents. In J. Gubrium & J. Holstein (Eds.), *Handbook of interview research* (pp. 181-201). Thousand Oaks, CA: Sage.

Elliott, D. S., Wilson, W. J., Huizinga, D., Sampson, R. J., Elliott, A., & Rankin, B. (1996). The effects of neighborhood disadvantage on adolescent development. *Journal of Research in Crime and Delinquency, 33*, 389-426.

Evans, W. P., Brown, R., & Killian, E. (2002). Decision making and perceived postdetention success among incarcerated youth. *Crime & Delinquency, 48*(4), 553-567.

Fagan, A. A. (2005). The relationship between adolescent physical abuse and criminal offending: Support for an enduring and generalized cycle of violence. *Journal of Family Violence, 20*(5), 279-290.

Fairey, T. (2010). *Therapeutic photography*. Retrieved March 21, 2010 from http://www.photovoice.org/html/methodology3tp/index.htm.

Fields, D. & Abrams, L. S. (2010). Gender differences in the perceived needs and barriers of youth offenders preparing for community reentry. *Child Youth Care Forum, 39*(4), 253-269.

Fiendholt, N. E., Michael, Y. L., & Davis, M. M. (2011). Photovoice engages rural youth in obesity prevention. *Public Health Nursing, 28*(2), 186-192.

Fletcher, A. (2006). *Washington youth voice handbook: The what, who, why, where, when, and how youth voice happens.* Olympia, WA: CommonAction.

Foley, R. M. (2001). Academic characteristics of incarcerated youth and correctional education programs: A literature review. *Journal of Emotional and Behavioral Disorders, 9,* 248-259.

Freeman, L. N., Mokros, H., & Poznanski, E. O. (1993). Violent events reported by normal urban school-aged children: Characteristics and depression correlates. *Journal of the American Academy of Child and Adolescent Psychiatry, 32,* 419-423.

Freire, P. (2005). *Pedagogy of the oppressed.* New York: The Continuum International Publishing Group Ltd. (Original work published 1970/1995).

Fryer, S. L., Crocker, N. A., & Mattson, S. N. (2008). Exposure to teratogenic agents as a risk factor for psychopathology, In T. P. Beauchaine, & S. P. Hinshaw (Eds.), *Child and adolescent psychopathology* (pp. 180-207). Hoboken, NJ: John Wiley & Sons.

Gallagher, C. A. (1999). *Juvenile offenders in residential placement, 1997.* Washington, DC: Office of Juvenile Justice and Delinquency Prevention.

Gemignani, R. J. (1994). *Juvenile correctional education: A time for change.* Retrieved from http://www.ncjrs.gov/pdffiles/juved.pdf.

Goldkind, L. (2011). A leadership opportunity for school social workers: Bridging the gaps in school reentry for juvenile justice system youths. *Children & Schools, 33*(4), 229-239.

Hanna, F. J., Hanna, C. A., & Keys, S. G. (1999). Fifty strategies for counseling defiant, aggressive adolescents: Reaching, accepting, and relating. *Journal of Counseling & Development, 77*(4), 395-404.

Hanna, F. J., Talley, W. B., & Guindon, M. H. (2000). The power of oppression: Toward a model of cultural oppression and liberation. *Journal of Counseling & Development, 78,* 430-441.

Heaven, P. C. L., Newbury, K., & Mak, A. (2004). The impact of adolescent and parental characteristics on adolescent levels of delinquency and depression. *Personality and Individual Differences, 36,* 173-185.

Horton, A. M., Jr., & Horton, A. M., III. (2005). Understanding the neuropsychology of drug abuse. In R. C. D'Amato, E. Fletcher-Janzen, & C. R. Reynolds (Eds.), *Handbook of school neuropsychology* (pp. 596-613). Hoboken, NJ: John Wiley & Sons.

Huffine, C. (2006). *Bad conduct, defiance, and mental health.* FOCAL POINT Research, Policy, and Practice in Children's Mental Health. Retrieved from www.rtc.pdx.edu.

Inderbitzin, M. (2009). Reentry of emerging adults: Adolescent inmates' transition back into the community. *Journal of Adolescent Research, 24*(4), 453-476.

Jimerson, S. R. (1999). On the failure of failure: Examining the association between early grade retention and education and employment outcomes during late adolescence. *Journal of School Psychology, 37*, 243-272.

Katsiyannis, A., & Archwamety, A. (1997). Factors related to recidivism among delinquent youths in a state correctional facility [Electronic version]. *Journal of Child and Family Studies, 6*(1), 43-55.

Keilitz, I., & Dunivant, N. (1986). The relationship between learning disability and juvenile delinquency: Current state of knowledge. *Remedial and Special Education, 7*, 18-26.

Kupersmidt, J. B., DeRosier, M. E., & Patterson, C. P. (1995). Similarity as the basis for children's friendships: The roles of sociometric status, aggressive and withdrawn behavior, academic achievement and demographic characteristics. *Journal of Social and Personal Relationships, 12*, 439-452. Retrieved September 14, 2006, from SAGE database.

Lane, J., Lanza-Kaduce, L., Frazier, C. E., & Bishop, D. M. (2002). Adult versus juvenile sanctions: Voices of incarcerated youths [Electronic version]. *Crime & Delinquency, 48*(3), 431-455.

Larson, K. A. (1988). A research review and alternative hypothesis explaining the link between learning disability and delinquency. *Journal of Learning Disabilities, 21*(6), 357-369.

Lawrence, R. (2007). *School crime and juvenile justice.* New York: Oxford University Press.

Lawrence, R. & Hesse, M. (2010). *Juvenile justice: The essentials.* CA: Sage.

Leone, P. E. (1994). Education services for youth with disabilities in a state-operated juvenile correctional system: Case study and analysis. *The Journal of Special Education, 28*, 43-58.

Leone, P. E., & Cutting, C. A. (2004). Appropriate education, juvenile corrections, and No Child Left Behind. *Behavioral Disorders, 29*(3), 260-265.

Leone, P. E., Krezmien, M., Mason, L., & Meisel, S. M. (2005). Organizing and delivering empirically based literacy instruction to incarcerated youth. *Exceptionality, 13*(2), 89-102.

Lorenz, L. S. (2010). Visual metaphors of living with brain injury: Exploring and communicating lived experience with an invisible injury. *Visual Studies, 25*(3), 210-223.

Lyon, R. G., Fletcher, J. M., & Fuchs, L. S. (2006). Learning disabilities. In E. J. Mash & R. A. Barkley (Eds.), *Treatment of childhood disorders* (3rd ed., pp. 512-591). New York: Guilford Press.

Macallair, D. (1993). Reaffirming rehabilitation in juvenile justice. *Youth & Society, 25*, 104-125.

Malmgren, K., Abbott, R. D., & Hawkins, J. D. (1999). LD and delinquency: Rethinking the "link." *Journal of Learning Disabilities, 32*, 194-200.

Marcus, R. F., & Sanders-Reio, J. (2001). The influence of attachment on school completion. *School Psychology Quarterly, 16*, 427-444.

Masten, A. S. (2001). Ordinary magic: Resilience processes in development. *American Psychologist, 56*(3), 227-238.

Matvya, J., Lever, N. A., & Boyle, R. (2006, August). *School reentry of juvenile offenders*. Baltimore, MD: Center for School Mental Health Analysis and Action, Department of Psychiatry, University of Maryland School of Medicine.

McCabe, K. M., Hough, R. L., Yeh, M., Lucchini, S. E., & Hazen, A. (2005). The relation between violence exposure and conduct problems among adolescents: A prospective study. *American Journal of Orthopsychiatry, 75*, 575-584.

Mears, D. P., Ploeger, M., & Warr, M. (1998). Explaining the gender gap in delinquency: Peer influence and moral evaluations of behavior. *Journal of Research in Crime and Delinquency, 35*, 251-266.

Mears, D. P., & Travis, J. (2004). Youth development and reentry. *Youth Violence and Juvenile Justice, 2*(1), 3-20.

Meisels, S. J., & Liaw, F. R. (1993). Failure in grade: Do retained students catch up? *Journal of Educational Research, 87*, 69-77.

Merriam, S. B. (1998). *Qualitative research and case study applications in education.* San Francisco: Jossey-Bass.

Mincey, B., Maldonado, N., Lacey, C. H., & Thompson. (2008). Perceptions of successful graduates of juvenile residential programs: Reflections and suggestions for success. *The Journal of Correctional Education, 59*(1), 8-31.

Moffitt, T. E. (1993). Adolescence-limited and life-course-persistent antisocial behavior: A developmental taxonomy. *Psychological Review, 100*, 674-701.

Mrug, S., Hoza, B., & Bukowski, W. M. (2004). Choosing or being chosen by aggressive-disruptive peers: Do they contribute to children's externalizing and internalizing problems? *Journal of Abnormal Child Psychology, 32*, 53-65.

Murray, J., & Farrington, D. P. (2005). Parental imprisonment: Effect on boys' antisocial behaviour and delinquency through the life-course. *Journal of Child Psychology and Psychiatry, 46*, 1269-1278.

Murray, J., & Farrington, D. P. (2010). Risk factors for Conduct Disorder and delinquency: Key findings from longitudinal studies. *The Canadian Journal of Psychiatry, 55*(10), 633-642.

Nangle, D. W., Erdley, C. A., & Gold, J. A. (1996). A reflection on the popularity construct: The importance of who likes or dislikes a child. *Behavior Therapy, 27*, 337-352.

National Association of School Psychologists. (2011a). Grade retention and social promotion (Position Statement). Bethesda, MD: Author.

National Association of School Psychologists, (2011b). Grade retention and social promotion. (White paper). Bethesda, MD: Author

Nelson, C. M. (2000). Educating students with emotional and behavioral disabilities in the 21st century: Looking through windows, opening doors. *Education and Treatment of Children, 23*(3), 204-225. Retrieved December 27, 2005, from Infotrack database.

Office of Juvenile Justice and Delinquency Prevention. (2004). *Model programs guide.* Retrieved March 30, 2012 from http://www.ojjdp.gov/mpg.

Patchin, J. W., Huebner, B. M., McCluskey, J. D., Varano, S. P., & Bynum, T. S. (2006). Exposure to community violence and childhood delinquency. *Crime and Delinquency, 52*, 307-332.

Perry, B. D. (1994). *The effects of traumatic events on children: Materials for parents.* Retrieved from http://www.childtrauma.org/ctamaterials/effects.asp.

Perry, B. D. (2004). Maltreatment and the developing child: How early childhood experience shapes child and culture. *Inaugural Margaret McCain Lecture.* Retrieved from www.lfcc.on.ca.

Perry, B. D., & Pollard, R. (1998). Homeostasis, stress, trauma, and adaptation: A neurodevelopmental view of childhood trauma. *Child and Adolescent Psychiatric Clinics of North America, 7*(1), 33-51.

Perry, B. D., & Szalavitz, M. (2006). *The boy who was raised as a dog: And other stories from a child psychologist's notebook: What traumatized children can teach us about loss, love, and healing.* New York: Basic Books.

Peterson-Badali, M., & Broeking, J. (2009). Parents' involvement in the youth justice system: A view from the trenches. *Canadian Journal of Criminology and Criminal Justice, 51*(2), 255-270.

Pike, K. L. (1967). *Language in relation to a unified theory of the structure of human behavior.* The Hague: Mouton.

Pullmann, M. D., Kerbs, J., Koroloff, N., Veach-White, E., Gaylor, R., & Sieler, D. (2006). Juvenile offenders with mental health needs: Reducing recidivism using wraparound. *Crime and Delinquency, 52*(3), 375-397.

Puzzanchera, C., & Adams, B. (2011). *Juvenile arrests 2009.* Washington DC: U.S. Department of Justice, Office of Juvenile Justice and Delinquency Prevention (NCJ 236477).

Quinn, M. M., Rutherford, R. B., Leone, P. E., Osher, D. M., & Poirier, J. M. (2005). Youth with disabilities in juvenile corrections: A national survey. *Council for Exceptional Children, 71*(3), 339-345.

Rafoth, M. A. (2002). Best practices in preventing academic failure and promoting alternatives to retention. In A. Thomas & J. Grimes (Eds.), *Best practices in school psychology IV* (pp. 789-798). Bethesda, MD: National Association of School Psychologists.

Research & Evaluation Unit, Division of Youth Corrections. (2007). *Recidivism evaluation of committed youth discharged in Fiscal Year 2004-05.* Retrieved March 29, 2010 from http://www.cdhs.state.co.us/dyc/PDFs/Recidivism_Jan2007.pdf.

Research & Evaluation Unit, Division of Youth Corrections. (2012). *Recidivism evaluation of committed youth discharged in Fiscal Year 2009-10.* Retrieved April 25, 2012 from http://www.colorado.gov/cdhsdyc/Resources-Publications/Recid2012.pdf.

Rogers, M. R., & O'Bryon, E. C. (2008). Advocating for social justice: The context for change in school psychology. *School Psychology Review, 37*(4), 493-498.

Rosler, M. (1989). In, around, and afterthoughts (on documentary photography). In R. Bolton (Ed.), *The contest of meaning* (pp. 303-342). Cambridge, MA: MIT Press.

Roy-Stevens, C. (2004). Overcoming barriers to school reentry. *OJJDP Fact Sheet, October*(3).

Rutherford, R. B., Nelson, C. M., & Wolford, B. I. (1985). Special education in the most restrictive environment: Correctional/special education. *The Journal of Special Education, 19*(1), 59-71.

Scarpa, A. (2003). Community violence exposure in young adults. *Trauma, Violence, & Abuse, 4*, 210-227.

Shaw, C. R. & McKay, H. (1969). *Juvenile delinquency and urban areas.* Chicago: University of Chicago Press. (Original work published 1942).

Shoemaker, D. J. (2000). *Theories of delinquency: An examination of delinquent behavior* (4th ed.). New York: Oxford University Press.

Sirpal, S. K. (1997). Causes of gang participation and strategies for prevention in gang members' own words. *Journal of gang research, 4*(2), 13-22.

Skovdal, M. (2011). Picturing the coping strategies of caregiving children in Western Kenya: From images to action. *Images of Health, 101*(3), 452-453.

Snyder, H. N. (2004). An empirical portrait of the youth reentry population. *Youth Violence and Juvenile Justice, 2*, 39-55.

Snyder, H. N. (2006). *Juvenile arrests 2004.* Washington, DC: U.S. Department of Justice, Office of Juvenile Justice and Delinquency Prevention (NCJ 214563).

Snyder, H., & Mulako-Wantota, J., Bureau of Justice Statistics, *Arrest Data Analysis Tool* [online, released 09/22/2011].

Snyder, H. N., & Sickmund, M. (1999). *Juvenile offenders and victims: 1999 national report.* Washington, DC: U.S. Department of Justice, Office of Juvenile Justice and Delinquency Prevention.

Snyder, H. N., & Sickmund, M. (2006). *Juvenile offenders and victims: 2006 national report.* Washington, DC: U.S. Department of Justice, Office of Juvenile Justice and Delinquency Prevention.

Spencer, M. B., & Jones-Walker, C. (2004). Interventions and services offered to former juvenile offenders reentering their communities: An analysis of program effectiveness. *Youth Violence and Juvenile Justice, 2*(1), 88-97.

Strack, R. W., Magill, C., & McDonagh, K. (2004). Engaging youth through Photovoice. *Health Promotion Practice, 5*, 49-58.

Sullivan, M. L. (2004). Youth perspectives on the experience of reentry. *Youth Violence and Juvenile Justice, 2*(1), 56-71.

Sullivan, T. N., Farrell, A. D., & Kliewer, W. (2006). Peer victimization in early adolescence: Association between physical and relational victimization an drug use, aggression, and delinquent behaviors among urban middle school students. *Development and Psychopathology, 18*, 119-137.

Teachman, J. D., Paasch, K., & Carver, K. (1997). Social capital and the generation of human capital. *Social Forces, 75*, 1343-1359.

Thornberry, T. P., Freeman-Gallant, A., Lizotte, A. J., Krohn, M. D., & Smith, C. A. (2003). Linked lives: The intergenerational transmission of antisocial behavior. *Journal of Abnormal Child Psychology, 31*(2), 171-185.

Thornberry, T. P., Smith, C. A., Rivera, C., Huizinga, D., & Stouthamer-Loeber, M. (1999). *Family disruption and delinquency.* Washington, DC: U.S. Department of Justice, Office of Juvenile Justice and Delinquency Prevention.

Todis, B., Bullis, M., Waintrup, M., Schultz, R., & D'Ambrosio, R. (2001). Overcoming the odds: Qualitative examination of resilience among formerly incarcerated adolescents. *Exceptional Children, 68*(1), 119-139.

Vaughan, C. (2010). "When the road is full of potholes, I wonder why they are bringing condoms?" Social spaces for understanding Papua New Guineans' health-related knowledge and health-promoting action. *AIDS Care, 22*(Supplement 2), 1644-1651.

Walker-Barnes, C. J., & Mason, C. A. (2004). Delinquency and substance use among gang-involved youth: The moderating role of parenting practices. *American Journal of Community Psychology, 34*, 235-250.

Wang, C. (2005). Method. In *Photovoice: Social change through photography*. Retrieved September 20, 2008 from http://www.photovoice.com/method/ index.html.

Wang, C. C., & Burris, M. A. (1994). Empowerment through Photovoice: Portraits of participation. *Health Education Quarterly, 21*, 171-186.

Wang, C., & Burris, M. A. (1997). Photovoice: Concept, methodology, and use for participatory needs assessment. *Health Education & Behavior, 24*, 369-387.

Wang, C., Burris, M. A., & Ping, X. Y. (1996). Chinese village women as visual anthropologists: A participatory approach to reaching policymakers. *Social Sciences & Medicine, 42*, 1391-1400.

Wang, C. C., Cash, J. L., & Powers, L. S. (2000). Who knows the streets as well as the homeless? Promoting personal and community action through Photovoice. *Health Promotion Practice, 1*, 81-89.

Wang, C. C., Morrel-Samuels, S., Hutchison, P. M., Bell, L., & Pestronk, R. M. (2004). Flint photovoice: Community building among youths, adults, and policymakers. *American Journal of Public Health, 94*(6), 911-913.

Wang, C. C., & Redwood-Jones, Y. A. (2001). Photovoice ethics: Perspectives from Flint Photovoice. *Health Education & Behavior, 28*, 560-572.

Wang, X., Blomberg, T. G., & Li, S. D. (2005). Comparison of the educational deficiencies of delinquent and nondelinquent students. *Evaluation Review, 29*(4), 291-312.

Warr, M. (1993). Parents, peers, and delinquency. *Social Forces, 72*(1), 247-264.

Warr, M. (2000). Fear and crime in the United States: Avenues for research and policy. In D. Duffee (Ed.), *Criminal justice 2000* (Volume 4: Measurement and analysis of crime and justice; pp. 451-489). Washington, DC: U.S. Department of Justice: National Institute of Justice (NCJ 182411).

Wheldall, K., & Watkins, R. (2004). Literacy levels of male juvenile justice detainees. *Educational Review, 56*(1), 3-11.

White, K. J., Rubin, E. C., & Graczyk, P. A. (2002). Aggressive children's perceptions of behaviorally similar peers: The influence of one's own behavioral characteristics on perceptions of deviant peers. *Journal of Social and Personal Relationships, 19*, 755-775.

Widom, C. S., & Maxfield, M. G. (2001). National Institute of Justice Research in brief: An update on the "cycle of violence". Washington, DC: U.S. Department of Justice.

Wilson, W. W., Stover, C. S., & Berkowitz, S. J. (2009). Research review: The relationship between childhood violence exposure and juvenile antisocial behavior: A meta-analytic review. *Journal of Child Psychology and Psychiatry, 50*(7), 769-779.

Wilson, K. J. (2008). Literature review: Wraparound services for juvenile and adult offender populations. *Center for Public Policy Research*, 1-15.

Wilson, N., Dasho, S., Martin, A. C., Wallerstein, N., Wanc, C. C., & Minkler, M. (2007). Engaging young adolescents in social action through photovoice: The youth empowerment strategies (YES!) project. *The Journal of Early Adolescence, 27*(2), 241-261.

Wood, R. J., Wood, A. R., & Mullins, D. T. (2008). Back to school: Recommendations to assist mentally ill, post-incarcerated youth return to school. *Journal of School Health, 78*(9), 514-517.

Wyoming Photovoice. (n.d.). Retrieved October 5, 2007 from http://web.me.com/wyobecker/Photovoice/Home.html.

Zabel, R. H., & Nigro, F. A. (1999). Juvenile offenders with behavioral disorders, learning disabilities, and no disabilities: Self-reports of personal, family, and school characteristics. *Behavioral Disorders, 25*, 22-40.

Zamora, D. (2005). Levels of academic achievement and further delinquency among detained youth. *The Southwest Journal of Criminal Justice, 2*, 1-16.

Ziedenberg, J. (2011). You're an adult now: Youth in adult criminal justice systems. Washington DC: U.S. Department of Justice, National Institute of Corrections.

Index